Misfit MOGUL

Misfit
MOGUL

AN OUTSIDER'S
TRANSFORMATION FROM
invisible
TO
innovator

Hisham Ahmad

Forbes | Books

Published by Forbes Books, Charleston, South Carolina.
An imprint of Advantage Media Group.

Forbes Books is a registered trademark, and the Forbes Books colophon is a trademark of Forbes Media, LLC.

Printed in the United States of America.

10 9 8 7 6 5 4 3 2 1

ISBN: 979-8-88750-582-4 (Hardcover)
ISBN: 979-8-88750-338-7 (Paperback)
ISBN: 979-8-88750-339-4 (eBook)

Library of Congress Control Number: 2023924215

Cover design by Analisa Smith.
Layout design by Lance Buckley.

This custom publication is intended to provide accurate information and the opinions of the author in regard to the subject matter covered. It is sold with the understanding that the publisher, Forbes Books, is not engaged in rendering legal, financial, or professional services of any kind. If legal advice or other expert assistance is required, the reader is advised to seek the services of a competent professional.

Since 1917, Forbes has remained steadfast in its mission to serve as the defining voice of entrepreneurial capitalism. Forbes Books, launched in 2016 through a partnership with Advantage Media, furthers that aim by helping business and thought leaders bring their stories, passion, and knowledge to the forefront in custom books. Opinions expressed by Forbes Books authors are their own. To be considered for publication, please visit **books.Forbes.com**.

To all the Outsiders of the world .

*You're young, pissed off, and confused, but you
will change the world with your brilliant ideas*

CONTENTS

ACKNOWLEDGMENTS

I'd like to thank my dad for not killing me after reading this book, but I'm still not sure of the outcome, so I'm writing this with desperate hope.

To Mr. Faizan, thank you for teaching me all the boring-ass shit that made me rich and has helped me teach others. You always believed in me and have talked on the phone with me past that awkward stage.

To the amazing team at Forbes Books, your dedication to bringing *Misfit Mogul* to life has inspired me and cost me a fortune. To my super brilliant editors, Annette Parks and Lauren Steffes, you helped my napkin ideas soar.

I'll say to my best friend, Rehan: You did nothing to make this book come to life. We FaceTimed, and you frequently busted my balls out of jealousy. Thanks to all my پاکستانی (Pakistani) friends and relatives, who will probably never speak to me again, and to the دیوی (Goddess) Maryam, who might also read this and never speak to me again. Or the opposite ...

On a more serious note, thanks again, Dad, for coming to America and allowing me the American dream. I know how much it meant to you, and it means a lot to me. Thanks to author Robert T. Kiyosaki. The journey has taught me that I have three rich dads with rich mindsets. Let's do this.

GLOSSARY OF TERMS

Life is messy, and being a kid is hard. Being an adult gets even harder. (Is that sincerely possible?) So I'm helping you out. Here are some words that I use throughout this book. Keep in mind that these are my own definitions. If you want to look them up in a dictionary, you'll first have to time travel to find one, or just ask your parents (although they probably don't own dictionaries anymore either).

Misfit: A crazy-ass kid with subversive thoughts and a warm heart.

Mogul: A person who gets rich through innovation and hard work.

Outsider: Someone who feels excluded from everyone else.

Invisible: Self-explanatory. You're not seen, even when you're young and rich.

Shit and Fuck: Words used often throughout the text.

Old School: The place where you're at right now. Tests, SATs, cramming knowledge you'll never use ... boredom.

New School: A change in mindset and teaching where you don't rely on outdated principles that train you to be a good employee.

Bro/Dude/Man: These terms refer to you, no matter your gender! I'm glad that you're here. I want to show you that you can become a success by stepping out of the box, feeling awkward, fucking up, and rising like a phoenix from the flames to reach your ultimate success.

Misfit Motivation: Musings of a Misfit that you might relate to.

Invisible Homework: Homework with no pressure attached. No one will see it or judge it.

Notes 'n' Stuff: A random place where you can write shit down.

INTRODUCTION

*I grew up being different, and
difference sparks innovation.*

I was slogging through the pages of my math book, feverishly writing notes. Closing my eyes tight, I allowed the information to fully sink in. My brain spun as numbers swirled behind my eyelids. My head hurt, and I massaged my temples, feeling on the verge of mental exhaustion. When I opened my eyes again, the soft light of my school library was blinding to my fourteen-year-old eyes.

In front of me sat ten different textbooks and a few books for pleasure, including Colin Wilson's *The Outsider*. The table wobbled from the weight of those words. My back ached from carrying the books to school. The pain didn't matter. I would learn *everything* and nail each test. I had the determination to go the extra mile and make it happen. I'd stay up all night if I had to, hiding in my bedroom with a flashlight and a prayer. (I had a strict curfew.)

PUSHING TOO HARD

It felt like I'd been in the silent library for hours, and I probably had. The tiny finance section with the Dewey Decimal categorization of 332.024 was at my back. I was intrigued by those finance books. I

1

could hear my father's voice: "The rich don't work for money." Well, that just didn't make sense. How would that help me in school?

I shook off the thought of those glossy paperbacks and turned my attention to my English textbook. American English would require even more cramming and notes. Since I was a skinny Islamic kid living in Texas, perfecting and excelling at this subject was my only hope of fitting in (which I didn't).

After filling my mind with grammar, syntax, and punctuation, I picked up a copy of English poems to execute what I thought was a "perfect" American accent.

EQUIPMENT

Figure it out for yourself, my lad,
You've all that the greatest of men have had,
Two arms, two hands, two legs, two eyes,
And a brain to use if you would be wise.
With this equipment they all began,
So start for the top and say: I can.

Look them over, the wise and great,
They take their food from a common plate
And similar knives and forks they use,
With similar laces they tie their shoes,
The world considers them brave and smart.
But you've all they had when they made their start.

Courage must come from the soul within,
The man must furnish the will to win,
So figure it out for yourself, my lad,
You were born with all that the great have had,
With your equipment they all began.
Get hold of yourself, and say: I can.

—EDGAR A. GUEST

The poem made perfect sense and got me dreaming about the future. What an incredible reminder that I had the same equipment that everyone else has. I worked harder than most, but this effort made me feel like I was spinning my wheels. Edgar A. Guest talked of "winning" and "I can," but was I *winning*? And *I can* do what in particular? The poem provided enthusiasm but no destination. It was similar to my dad's voice saying, "The rich don't work for money." What the heck did that mean, and how was I to make money anyhow?

──────────── | MISFIT MOTIVATION | ────────────

"You Can" is completely true We all have the same capabilities it's what you do with them that counts You're designed to be just as successful as anyone else

BACK TO REALITY

These questions quickly disappeared as the noontime school bell rang, and I ran to the window. It was easier to *watch* the other kids eat their lunches together in the quad. They could afford the oily pizza and french fries from the cafeteria, but I didn't have a cent in my pocket. My father knew better—we needed to save. Last night's Paki biryani was now lying cold in an old piece of Tupperware on my problematic library table—a once-sumptuous meal flavored with cumin, cinnamon, cardamom, cloves, garlic, and ginger was now a clumped, dried mess swimming in a pool of yogurt that I had to eat with a spork.

I kept watching the joyful kids sitting together at cement tables in the sunshine with their canned Coke and Sprite. They were dressed so well; it seemed like they all lived in palaces. My heart sank as I watched every person I wanted to be friends with laugh and chat together.

The prettiest girl in school, who was wearing a pink dress and beige hijab, caught my eye. I'd tried to talk to her once, and it didn't work out. She'd walked away like I was a ghost. Girls might not be in my future, I thought.

The happy-go-lucky scene outside started to make me angry—*rebellious*. I returned to the 332.024 section and saw a title that intrigued me: *Rich Dad Poor Dad*. I grabbed it fast and sat at my wobbly table to study even harder. My intensity and solitude made perfect sense. I'd rather have the highest GPA than be the sad, lonely kid that everyone ignored. If I didn't have friends, so be it. At least I'd be the best at something.

───── | MISFIT MOTIVATION | ─────

Not fitting in won't last for long. If these feelings are overwhelming, know that you're an Outsider for a reason—you think differently. That's your greatest gift. Head over to call number 332.024. Do it at a young age.

FATIGUE SETS IN

This spike in ambition was short-lived, as I felt a heat in my nose running down my lip. My frequent nosebleeds … I quickly reached into my backpack to grab the napkins I always carried with me. Many of them I'd already made sketches on when my mind was on overdrive. I brought a sketch of Mars to my bloody nostrils and held on tight.

As I sat in the library, mortified, wondering how to escape without being seen, an idea came to mind: *the unhinged table*. I'd make a sketch and figure out the *perfect* table. I grabbed a marker and tried to fix the problem on the back of a napkin that already had a T-shirt design I'd imagined. With one hand on my nose and the other on the marker, I drew the dimensions for a new table that was strong enough to bear the weight of my school insecurity and confusion.

This burst of creativity had a purpose behind it. I needed to waste time until the nosebleed stopped. When kids flooded into the library, I appeared busy, and they probably thought I had a bad cold. This smoke and mirrors worked for a while until the stuffy librarian passed my table as I continued to sketch.

-| MISFIT MOTIVATION |-
Librarians are scary

CAUGHT IN THE ACT

"Hisham!" The librarian placed her hand angrily on her hip. This wasn't the first time she caught me here or the last. Her cheeks were flaming red, and her customary No. 2 pencil was stuck in her silver bun like a bibliophile geisha.

"All the teachers said you didn't come to school today."

As she waited for a response, I blinked several times and chose my words carefully. "I've been at school this whole time, ma'am." It was common sense …

The librarian sat beside me with concern in her green eyes. "This has happened one too many times. You're top of your class, but you don't *go* to class."

"Because it's boring."

"Don't you understand, Hisham? This is the beginning of your future. Someday, you'll have to show up to a job!"

The librarian meant well, but what was the point of going to class when I could do it all by myself? Besides, I didn't want a normal job.

I wanted to draw out my ideas and eventually be the kid who *buys* everyone pizza.

I joked with her. "I'll become a librarian then."

She shook her head. "I'm telling the principal to call your father."

My heart pounded in my chest. This was the *last* thing that I wanted to have happen again. My father would be furious! "Please don't," I pleaded.

"I'm afraid it's necessary." She looked at my table sketch and rolled her eyes. "You daydream too much."

Pointing at the schematic drawing, I insisted with my young voice, "One day I will make this table, library lady." I lifted the copy of *Rich Dad Poor Dad* and handed it to her. "And I'd like to check out this book, ma'am."

"Oh, Hisham." She gazed down at my copy of Colin Wilson's book *The Outsider*. "You are the Outsider!"

For the first time in a while, I smiled.

It struck me that I was in the position of so many of my favourite characters in fiction: Dostoevsky's Raskolnikov, Rilke's Malte Laurids Brigge, the young writer in Hamsun's Hunger: alone in my room, feeling totally cut off from the rest of society. It was not a position I relished … Yet an inner compulsion had forced me into this position of isolation. I began writing about it in my journal, trying to pin it down. And then, quite suddenly, I saw that I had the makings of a book. I turned to the back of my journal and wrote at the head of the page: "Notes for a book The Outsider in Literature."

—COLIN WILSON, 1954

PART I

THE POWER OF
Invisibility

THE STORY THAT STARTED MANY

You're writing down napkin ideas for a reason

I tiptoed into the house, my SpongeBob backpack causing me to arch my spine in discomfort. The goal was to make it past my father's office and get upstairs to my room. I felt like crying. Even though I enjoyed the term *Outsider*, the loneliness was getting to me. If I could just retreat up those stairs, then playing *Dungeon Fighter* would clear my head.

I heard his familiar tone of voice. "Hisham."

Ahh! I brought my hand to my forehead just as the zipper of my backpack broke from the pressure. All my books and sketches came pouring out onto the Persian rug, as well as my "Rival Box," a series of sketches that I treasured most.

"Hey, Dad," I said with a forced smile.

My father stepped out of his office and shook his head in displeasure. "The principal called."

"I know, I know. But I was *at* school." As I knelt to collect my books and napkins (which appeared to have gone through a hurricane), my father stopped me.

"What is all of this, son?" He picked up a handful of sketches.

I'd never shown them to him before and became lightheaded, assuming my father would be furious. "It's what I do when I get bored."

His eyes narrowed. "You don't attend class, and then you sketch ideas all day?"

"I have to!" I argued. "I'm bored, Dad. I memorize the lessons so quickly, and then my head is overwhelmed. I'll probably never use this stuff." In the silence, I felt my cheeks turn red. I'd never spoken to my father like that before, but it was time to be honest. "I have all these ideas. I can't stop them. They wake me up in the morning, and I can see them when I'm sleeping at night. What I'm learning is important; I know that. But sometimes it feels like my imagination wants something else."

"Something else?"

"I want to *do* something. I feel like I'll go crazy if I can't *do* something."

| MISFIT MOTIVATION |

What you study in school is mind-numbingly boring.
*Decide early on that you want to **do** something with*
that knowledge How can it be applied to your dreams?

THE SHIFT

My father exhaled. "Listen. Listen, Hisham, I'm not surprised."

My eyes went wide with wonder. He understood! A tremendous weight was lifted from my shoulders.

"I was the same way." My father knelt to pick up the copy of *Rich Dad Poor Dad* that rested on top of my splayed math book. "In every sense."

My brain was dying of curiosity. It had been so hard to relate to my father up until this point, and now we connected on *something*—we shared a momentary understanding. "What did you do?" I asked.

I witnessed sadness in my father's eyes as he reflected. Never had he been so vulnerable in front of me. "I let it go."

Those four words hit me like a punch to the gut. "Why?"

He continued to stare at the face of Robert T. Kiyosaki, the author of *Rich Dad Poor Dad*, who appeared confident, jovial, and proud. "That's a very good question, my boy."

At that moment, I had a premonition that shook me to the core—the first glimmer of being understood, but it was more than that. I also understood *my father*. I could see in his eyes and expression that he had regrets. Granted, my father could be considered a very successful man by anyone's standards, but there was a piece missing for him, as there was for me.

"Is this a good book?" he asked.

"I don't know," I candidly replied. "I haven't read it yet."

"Why did you pick it up?"

"Because you always say the rich don't work for money, and honestly, I want to know what that means." More needed to be said. Something was crying out inside me. "Dad, I'm lonely at school. I write ideas on napkins that fill me with excitement, and I use them to hide nosebleeds—nosebleeds that I'm pretty sure are caused by stress."

He flipped through the pages. "I read this years ago."

"You did!" This was amazing. Another thing in common! A coincidence … or not?

"Yes."

"And it made you focus on success?" Rarely had I shared admiration for my father, but in this new point of connection, I could finally let him know.

My father shook his head. "Son, I could have gone further. I could have"—he glanced at my drawings—"believed in my napkin ideas. The rich don't work for money because they allow their napkin ideas to work for them. They innovate and turn their ideas into a future of wealth."

──────── | MISFIT MOTIVATION | ────────

Being an Outsider eventually makes you an insider. Don't be afraid to share your ideas with your parents or anyone else for that matter. What you have sketched or written down means something.

HEAD SPINNING, LIKE ALWAYS

I couldn't sleep that night. I looked out the window at the streetlamp that poured light into my window. I thought about how that light could have a better bulb and dim as the night drew on. I considered my table sketch and how better materials could carry the weight of too many school books for a young kid. I also looked at the stars and marveled at how the color of each one was an indication of its temperature. The hottest stars were blue white, like a smoldering campfire. The coolest were orange or red.

This got me thinking about the color spectrum and whether there could ever be a satellite that went far enough to get close to a star. Ah! I was spinning inside and threw a pillow over my face. My brain wouldn't stop. I eventually imagined the girl in the pink dress, and her beauty helped me to fall asleep. I dreamt of a meteor crashing into earth.

After waking up in a sweat, I came downstairs to marvel at an unexpected scene. I was used to my dad seated at the kitchen table with a newspaper in front of his face, sipping on potent black tea and a glass of orange juice. Those customary beverages were still on the table, but my finance book from 332.024 (I'd memorized that in my sleep) had already been dog-eared, and Dad appeared to be near the end.

"Son, I have an idea."

My hair spiked all over the place. I looked like a newly hatched chicken. Or a South Asian Einstein. "Okay," I responded, bleary and in need of food.

"I'm taking you out of school today."

My emotions couldn't be concealed. I brought my hand into a fist and gritted my teeth in victory.

Dad put up a sobering hand. "Now, now. Calm down. This isn't forever. This is for today."

I tempered my ridiculous exhilaration and calmly stood in attendance to hear my father's words. "Why today?"

He shared, "I've read this book again. I was up all night."

That made two of us.

"And there's someone I want you to meet. Someone I've admired for a long time."

In my prepubescent mind, I was hoping it would be Taylor Swift, but I pushed that thought away. My father did have connections, but perhaps not *those* kinds of connections.

With my feet firmly planted on the cold tile of the kitchen floor, I felt the same sensation from the evening before. *Something is changing. Something is happening.* "Whatever it is, I want to do it."

My father tossed the book onto the table and sipped his tea. "And so we're doing it."

———————— | MISFIT MOTIVATION | ————————

When your parents are being mysterious, they're just trying to control you Bro, you have no choice but to go with it until you turn eighteen

SOMETHING BIG IS HAPPENING

The drive to wherever the heck we were going had my brain on overdrive, which was no cause for alarm. I stared out the window and watched sidewalks crumbling and wanted to find the answer. Green trees were too sparse on one street, and I thought of ways to make that street more hospitable. On a certain lawn, children went back and forth on a swing that looked like it could crash at any moment. So many solutions came to mind for these problems.

When we pulled up to a nondescript white building that looked like a warehouse, my father turned to me and said, "I knew this was right for you, but I thought it was too soon."

I felt a nosebleed coming. Why was he being so cryptic? Was I joining the Mafia? "And this is … ?" I asked.

"STEM school. You need to make something of your thoughts. Use your hands, use your ideas."

I felt sick to my stomach. Here was yet another place where I'd spend the whole day in the library being an Outsider.

"I'm going in," I said with my best faux FBI voice. As I stepped out of the car, the situation suddenly seemed ridiculous. I popped my head through the open window of my dad's Volvo and asked, "Wait, you're not coming in with me?"

"No, son. They know you're here. Step inside with the assurance that you're on the path to being the man you will one day become."

Backing away, I began to choke up. The man I'd one day become? Who was that? This rite of passage might get all *Mission: Impossible* at any moment.

As my father's car drove off, I continued to back away until I tripped on the curb and fell on my back (the backpack provided enough cushion). It was then, staring at the sky, that I realized this situation could perhaps be a disaster. It was so much easier studying alone—so much easier cramming knowledge and keeping to myself.

—————————— | MISFIT MOTIVATION | ——————————

*You will trip and fall many times. Always make it look casual like it was your **choice**.*

—————————————————————————————————————

WALKING IN LIKE 007

I took a short nap on the ground before dusting myself off and proceeding. I'd heard of STEM before—science, technology, engineering, and mathematics—but as I approached the front desk, I had the sinking suspicion I was joining a secret society. The James Bond of Freemasonry.

"Can I help you?" the young receptionist with the blond bob asked.

I blushed for a moment because she was pretty. "I'm … I'm Hisham Ahmad," I tentatively said, my voice cracking.

She looked through her book and found my name. With a warm smile, she replied, "Welcome, Hisham. You're to be in room eleven."

That was an auspicious number, so as I walked down the hall to room eleven, my legs shaking as I clutched my SpongeBob backpack, I felt a glimmer of hope. I reached the hallowed room and gently turned the knob, cracking the door open to find at least twenty other kids turning and staring.

"Oh shit." (Dad would have killed me for saying this had he not sped off.)

I quickly attempted to close the door and run until I heard the teacher's voice call out, "Hisham!"

Opening the door again, I met the teacher's eyes. He stood in front of the whiteboard, and as far as I could tell, he looked like he could be a member of the Ahmad family. Was he my uncle?

"My name is Mr. Faizan."

I bowed my head. It seemed awkward. This wasn't feudal Japan, but I didn't know what else to do.

He motioned toward a communal table—not like a normal desk—perched high. Four other students sat on stools. How clever! That was better for sketching.

"Have a seat, Hisham, and welcome to our class."

As I made the endless journey to the communal table, I inspected the other students with my peripheral vision. They seemed to look at me warmly. That didn't take away the tightness in my chest. There was another student with a SpongeBob backpack. Okay, this might be great, I thought.

------------------------------ | MISFIT MOTIVATION | ------------------------------

We are better at technology than adults. We were born with it in our hands. Use this capability to keep evolving as technology evolves. Use STEM and computer science to give you priceless knowledge, but take it a step further. Create something new.

HOPE RESTORED

Once I was seated, the other students at my table greeted me with smiles.

"All right then," Mr. Faizan said, turning to the whiteboard. "Allow me to remind you of the fundamentals."

And just like I was watching history unfold in front of me, image by image, much of what Mr. Faizan shared that morning turned me into the teenage CEO that I am today.

He wrote in broad letters:

Believe in Your Ideas
Bring Your Ideas to Life
Continue the Practice of Making Your Ideas Happen
If You Fail Try Again
If You Win Create a Patent

One kid raised his hand. "Yes, Mikhail," Mr. Faizan said.

"Will it make me rich?"

The kids snickered again, but I truly wanted to know the answer to this.

Mr. Faizan rested upon his desk, exuding a warm smile. "Mikhail, it could potentially make you rich, but that's not the point, is it?"

Wait, wait, wait! I sort of assumed that was the point, just like Mikhail.

"It's not?" Mikhail asked. "My dad wants me to be rich."

Holy ... all right, this kid was going to be my friend.

Mr. Faizan went on. "You see, Mikhail, becoming rich is very nice, but it starts with innovation. If your focus is on earning money, you won't succeed because richness only comes from solving larger problems in the world. Of course, you won't become rich working at Walmart, but that doesn't mean we don't need those important workers.

"Innovation breeds success, naturally. You patent one of your ideas, and then the money is making itself. You invest that money, and it continues to grow. This is the secret of the rich. They only work for themselves. This program is designed for you to work for yourself as well by believing in your ideas and having the practical skill to make them happen in real life."

I thought I might pass out. Last night, when my backpack split open in front of my father, that was perhaps the best thing that had ever happened to me. This was what I needed. The dull throb in my head from cramming impractical knowledge in it disappeared into a cloud of hope. I knew deep in my bones that I was in the right place.

A girl at my table raised her hand. I tried not to stare. "Mr. Faizan, with my bicycle patent, I feel like I don't know what to do about business stuff. My dad doesn't know what to do either."

Wait, what?! This chick had a patent already?

Mr. Faizan returned to the whiteboard to answer her question.

———————— | MISFIT MOTIVATION | ————————

Bros and chicks are equally capable of winning at this game In fact, the girls are probably smarter... but we can all be Misfit Moguls.

KNOWLEDGE UNFOLDING

"Here's the answer, Alexa."

"My name is Alexis."

Mr. Faizan appeared flustered. "Shit, I'm sorry."

Mikhail nearly keeled over. "This class is so awesome."

Financial Literacy, Mr. Faizan wrote. "You're not taught this in school," he shared, snapping the cap on his marker. "You're not taught these principles at a young age. You don't need an MBA to invent, create, patent, and start a business sprung from your imagination." Mr. Faizan pointed to those two words on the board once more. "The majority of people do not have this fundamental understanding."

Oh, I had to … I lifted a shaky hand, and Mr. Faizan pointed to me.

"Yes, Hisham."

"Um …" Gulp. "Mr. Faizan, my father is an accountant, but I don't have this knowledge either." Alexis glanced at me, and I knew for sure that I'd mess this up. I opened my backpack and pulled out a few of my sketches. A few kids said, "Cool." "I know it's my first day, but like … I feel a little stupid. To be honest with you," I said with a laugh, "I want to be rich like Mikhail does."

Mikhail threw up his hand. "Bro!"

"But I also want to keep sketching. I want to do something with my mind and my hands. I guess … I guess I want to change the … um, world."

The room fell silent, and I wondered if I'd said too much. Did I sound lame? Self-centered?

Mr. Faizan finally spoke. "Hisham, take everything you can learn from your father. Gain this financial literacy. He has it. Study taxes. He certainly knows about that."

I had to ask: "Do you know my dad or something?"

He grinned. "He does my taxes." Through the students' laughter, Mr. Faizan said, "Come to my office after class, Hisham."

─────────── | MISFIT MOTIVATION | ───────────

Everyone wants to be wealthy, but wealth comes from fostering your creativity and curiosity. Don't lose it! We may be young, but we're the future, and we can change the world with our ideas. Lastly, always file your taxes.

AFFIRMATION

I tentatively opened the door to Mr. Faizan's office. As students exited the halls, I heard someone say, "Nice meeting you, Hisham!"

It was the girl from my table who'd said it. My whole body froze in panic. I gave an awkward wave. "Thanks, Alexa." She rolled her eyes, and I knocked on the office door.

"Come in, Hisham," Mr. Faizan requested.

Still in shock from having a girl speak to me, I looked around the room, trying to find my bearings. There were framed pictures all over the walls—Albert Einstein, the solar system, Nikola Tesla, the first landing on the moon, and an incredible drawing of a satellite that I approached to inspect further. "That is so cool."

Mr. Faizan's response was casual. "I drew it."

"What?!" I had to tone down my reaction. "Is that so?"

The noble teacher got up from his desk and stood beside me, looking at the satellite. "It is interesting how life works, Hisham. I studied to be a computer scientist, and now I'm a consultant for NASA engineers."

My mouth fell open. "And ... you're still a teacher?"

"Of course. It is my passion," he offered with a warm smile. "Come, let me show you around."

The first room in the STEM warehouse was filled with computers. The walls were lined with schematic drawings, and accompanying these were real-life incarnations of these drawings—a chair, a pot, a drone, a handbag, and there was even an animatronic dog ... I was in heaven.

My excitement overwhelmed me. I felt seen! I zipped open my backpack (which I'd fixed while coming up with a new idea to never have it rip again) and poured my sketches onto one of the empty tables.

"Mr. Faizan, this is crazy. There are so many things I want to create." My enthusiasm seemed embarrassing, but I couldn't hold it back.

He perused my sketches, picking up each one before moving on to the next. "Hisham, there's a reason your father brought you here."

"Yes?"

"Most certainly."

"Why hasn't anyone told me this before? Why have I been breaking my head with knowledge, acing all my exams, while feeling completely at a loss?" The question had burned in my mind for so long.

"I have an answer for you. But first, let's go to the garden."

"The garden?"

"It's where our students go to think. Nature is the catalyst for clearing the mind and fostering creativity."

──────── | MISFIT MOTIVATION | ────────

Gardens, beaches, and mountaintops will not clear your head. This is a myth. Those crazy thoughts do not go away. Even yoga can't do it, bro...

THE GARDEN OF CREATIVITY

As I followed Mr. Faizan, I had to wonder how this warehouse had a garden and how this oasis might inspire creativity. I spent all my time in the library with a nosebleed and a headache. Once we stepped outside, it all quickly made sense. The green trees and flowers lifted my spirit for five seconds.

Mr. Faizan and I sat on a bench, looking at the tranquil beauty. "You see, Hisham, you're a model student in every way. You could easily go on to college and earn a solid job that will last the rest of your life. But that's not what you want, is it?"

I had to consider the question. "I'd go crazy."

"Exactly. You need to *create*, young man. Not only do you need to do this with your mind"—Mr. Faizan pointed to his forehead—"but also with your hands. And once you've done so, you can step away and reap the benefits of your creation."

The whole money topic had come up again, and I had to ask, "So, get rich from what I create?"

"If your purpose is to get rich, you'll always live in fear. True richness comes from your mind, sketches, and the practical knowledge that brings your ideas to life. Do not waste time. A good idea must be executed as quickly as possible. And wealth comes from this acumen." Mr. Faizan motioned out toward the luscious garden. "Having an open space in the *mind* from an early age. Believing in your ideas and letting them cascade through you while quickly learning how to transform them into reality."

My mind wandered to my table sketch. "But I don't know how to build."

"That's what we do here, young man. Twenty-five percent of our time is spent on theory, and 75 percent is spent on practice. You'll work every day to learn how to practically create things in the real world. This is what's lost in our educational system."

I could have jumped up and danced. "So, I can stop going to school?"

Mr. Faizan laughed. "No, school is *necessary*. It's all theory, but it's still opening your mind. It's teaching you how to *learn*. Use it, but understand that it's setting you up to be a good employee. The schedule is the same if you worked at any job. What I'm seeing is that you have something bigger to offer, Hisham. You have a hunger for creativity and innovation, and from your sketches, I understand that your mind *does indeed* have the power to change the world."

I had to joke. "So, that will get me a girlfriend and a Lamborghini?"

Mr. Faizan brought a hand to his face and shook his head in dismay. "No, no. This is not the point." He finally relented. "Okay, most likely a girlfriend. But, listen—this is important: Displaying your wealth and spending money on frivolous things will bring you no happiness. Wealth only increases the fear of the rich man—paying bills, putting money on display, wanting more and more. Yes, you must make money, but one day, money can work for you."

Robert T. Kiyosaki spoke from the heavens: *The rich don't work for money.*

I couldn't help but feel like I was ahead of the game.

"Can I come back tomorrow?"

"Yes, after school."

Damn. "Yes, I will come."

As I got up to leave, Mr. Faizan shared one last thing. "Hisham, I believe in you. You're one of the brightest kids I've ever met."

"Thanks, I've always felt like such a loner."

"You're not a loner; you're an Outsider."

There was that word again.

———————— | MISFIT MOTIVATION | ————————

Our brains are soaking up ideas like a sponge There's no limit to what we can learn at this time in life Don't let this go Soak up everything that you can and turn it into action Gain a financial education at a young age and you will one day become your own boss

I learned some incredible lessons early on. When we're young, we have so many ideas, but school doesn't teach us practical knowledge. We must go elsewhere to find these lessons that allow us to truly know how to create what's in our heads. When you have your personal "napkin ideas," you might feel at a loss for how to *create* what you're dreaming of and then one day turn it into a business.

I share Mr. Faizan's ideas on financial education because we're not taught that in school. We're taught to be good employees and are terrified about money all our lives. This chapter highlights how starting young and investing in your ideas can lead you down a different path—a path of prosperity. But again, money is not the goal. If you're only focused on money, you'll always be afraid of losing it or not making enough. Money is not the point. Gain a financial education but also let your desire for money go.

Sure, patenting a product that changes the world will quickly give you a fancy car, but that's not the heart and soul of what an Outsider does. An Outsider thinks out of the box, starts learning about finances and business early, and primarily, believes in their ideas despite all the natural challenges that arise when bringing those ideas to life.

I came to life in STEM school, and Mr. Faizan's encouragement helped me to become the innovator and CEO that I am today. This was only the beginning of the story, and the graphic below introduces you to all the insane hurdles that came next. This is the process of analyzing a problem, asking questions, finding solutions, and then questioning those solutions. It's New School, real-life work.

Phases	Action Items	Timeline (in session)										
		1	2	3	4	5	6	7	8	9	10	11
Identification of a problem	Listing down problems and selecting top 5 (1 primary and 4 back up)	■										
	Starbursting and write problem statement of all problems		■									
	Conduct STAR analysis for all 5 problems			■								
	Conduct Root Cause Analysis (Identify weakest link in the problem chain					■						
Innovation Life Cycle	Identify and analyze all existing solutions						■					
	Brainstorm ideas to solve the problem (Fix the gap)							■				
Ideation / Innovation	Technical feasibility analysis								■			
	Patentability analysis									■		
	If patented/not feasible, go to backup problem and repeat Innovation Life Cycle										■	
	Finalize innovation										■	■

Invisible Homework

After each chapter, write down your thoughts. Think of Leonardo da Vinci. He needed to sketch everything, and those napkin ideas changed the world. The genius mind must write it down. The notes section can become a place for your napkin ideas or general thoughts about my weird Outsider life.

Notes 'n' Stuff:

(2)

DREAMING + REALITY = CONFUSION

*Sometimes, you'll feel like a bird falling
from the sky. You dream big, face reality,
and then get confused about how these two
coalesce. The Misfit Mogul isn't deterred.*

I woke up in a pool of sweat. The thought of returning to school that day sent my nervous system into overdrive. Back to reality ... I hosed myself off in the shower and came downstairs wearing a Ralph Lauren polo shirt that my dad had purchased from an outlet store. I thought the shirt was lame, but Dad would be pissed if I wore anything else. "Look the part," he always said. Well, which part was I playing, for fuck's sake? (My only Outsider redemption was that every shirt I owned had holes in it.)

"Did you sleep well, son?" my father asked from behind his newspaper.

I had to lie. "I did."

In truth, my return to regular school had me freaked out all night. I'd tossed and turned, contemplating that streetlamp again—how to make it less bright as the hours went on. Then I thought of a satellite like Mr. Faizan's. I'd sketched it around 4:00 a.m. If I made this idea happen, I'd be a millionaire.

"I'll pick you up from school and take you to STEM," my father said casually.

I smiled. The very notion of going back to STEM lifted my spirits. "Cool," I said flatly, hiding my excitement.

The Tupperware containing last night's samosas sat ready for me. My heart sank again because I knew I'd have to eat in secrecy instead of heating my food and subjecting my peers to the immaculate aroma of Paki food. Quickly stuffing the lunch into my backpack, I rushed to the door and then froze. "Father?" I asked.

He lowered his newspaper and gave me a discerning look. "Yes, Hisham?"

"I want to learn … um. It's what Mr. Faizan mentioned!" I searched for the words. "*Financial literacy.*"

"Why?"

"For when I become a millionaire." Let's just call that one moment of deeply introverted confidence …

The pause seemed endless. Dad looked off into the distance as though he was about to espouse the words of the Almighty. "I have a book for you," he finally replied. "You shared your book with me, and now I'll share mine."

—————— | MISFIT MOTIVATION | ——————

Never be afraid to ask people for guidance
Sometimes it's sucky guidance (if it's not from your
rich dad) but reaching out to others is key

LET THE TRAUMA BEGIN

I sped on my bike with my father's copy of *Federal Income Taxation: A Law Student's Guide to the Leading Cases and Concepts* tucked under my arm. The title was a mouthful, but I wanted to learn. I wanted to absorb everything my father could share with me. (And of course, I was hoping there was a chapter on how to make enough for a Lambo. Maybe even a chapter on dating.)

The great threat of having a new book to memorize was that I'd sit in the library alone once more, terrified and unable to interact with my peers. This proved true. Lunchtime came, and I stepped closer to the library window, watching the girl in the pink dress—today the girl in the purple dress and hijab (with sequins)—looking better every day. It was torture.

"Hisham!" There was the librarian again, angrier than the day before and now with a pen in her bun instead of a pencil. She'd evolved since I last received her anger. "This situation will not change." She wrapped her arms around her marigold sweatshirt and shook her head. "I want to see you connect with those other kids," the library lady vehemently requested. She pointed out the window. "Now!"

Okay, I was scared. I quickly gathered my copy of *Federal Income Taxation* as well as Colin Wilson's *The Outsider*.

"You will pay for this!" I exclaimed with some flare and then ran for my life. I guess I was trying to be a *Star Wars* character or something. I still don't have the answer to this outburst …

When I got down the stairs, through the door, and into the quad, I was out of breath and felt all eyes on me. I had to admit that there was a reason the librarian requested that I take a social leap—I was no longer in my comfort zone. The Outsider was on full display.

——————————— | MISFIT MOTIVATION | ———————————

If you're an Outsider in school—the geek, the nerd, the one who doesn't fit in—make the effort anyway. Even if you fail, you will have tried. As

*you'll soon learn, connecting with others is the
key to success and innovation. It might be hard.
Do it anyway. Don't keep yourself in a box.*

STEPPING OUT AND QUICKLY RETREATING

Escaping the discomfort of being stared at and judged, I opened *Rich Day, Poor Dad* (while clutching the taxation book for dear life) and ate my sad, cold samosa like it was Wagyu beef.

Mr. Kiyosaki wrote: "Decisiveness. The world is moving faster and faster. Stock market trades are made in milliseconds. Deals come and go on the Internet in a matter of minutes. More and more people are competing for good deals. So the faster you can make a decision, the more likely you'll be able to seize opportunities—before someone else does."[1]

It's what Mr. Faizan had said. Continue with your napkin ideas and learn early in life how to make them happen. *Decisiveness.* Looking up and witnessing the ملاك (Angel) of my demise, I was decisive about sketching the brown-skinned goddess in the purple dress. As I began to contemplate a new design for her outfit (the dress was too short, but I wasn't complaining), I felt a cup of ice-cold soda crash into my back.

I turned to try and see who had committed the crime before awkwardly pretending like nothing had happened. My heart broken, I gathered my things and walked away as calmly as I could, catching the purple-dress girl's eyes. Her hijab was black today. Maybe she was in mourning for my very existence.

---

1   Robert Kiyosaki, *Rich Dad Poor Dad: What the Rich Teach Their Kids About Money That the Poor and Middle Class Do Not!* (Scottsdale: Plata Publishing, 1997).

Bullying is real. We all get it in some way. If this is happening to you, I suggest that you run. Seriously, just run (or awkwardly walk). Wait for the day when you're the Misfit Mogul and have a bodyguard.

HEAVEN

I arrived early to an empty classroom. The quad had felt like being alone in a rain forest at night with red eyes in all directions. My back was still wet, but in the spirit of being an Outsider, I'd just sit at my desk dumbfounded and numb as though nothing had happened.

Kids started to file in, and I froze even more, reading the next chapter of *Rich Dad Poor Dad*, which I'd plastered in Marvel Comic stickers so no one could see the cover. Superman soared over the purple and gold design, unfortunately punching poor Mr. Kiyosaki in the face. I continued to read.

"Job security meant everything to my educated dad. Learning meant everything to my rich dad."[2]

Learning? What the … ? I looked down at the taxation book and frowned. What good would any of this *learning* do me?

My nervous (and somewhat fake) concentration broke when I felt someone eagerly sit at the desk to my right. I desperately hoped it wasn't the guy who threw the cup of soda, which I could now identify as Mountain Dew.

I felt him lean over and speak in a whisper. "Bro."

A greeting of *bro* could either be perilous or promising. What I discovered was another brown kid with large, warm eyes and a shaggy mane of black hair.

---

2   Kiyosaki, *Rich Dad Poor Dad*.

"Hey," I whispered back like we were both part of some kind of Islamic reconnaissance mission.

"I don't see you around much." He presented his fist for a bump. I met his fist in shaky silence, literally not able to create words but thankful for the gesture. "I'm Rehan. I saw what they did, man." Rehan pointed to my wet back. "That sucked!"

"Yeah."

Rehan reached into his bag and placed his copy of the Quran on his desk.

Hell momentarily turned into سماء (Arab heaven).

I was not religious, but there was something comforting about meeting someone like me in Texas. Literally, why were we South Asian people even here? I asked myself this question several times when I ran out of inventions.

I had to respond to his comment about my wet Ralph Lauren polo shirt with an air of confidence. "I don't really feel it."

"Why you never in class much, bro?"

I could tell the truth or lie. I went with the truth. "I already memorized the math lessons."

Rehan smiled broadly. "Dude, you fascinate me."

That was the moment I knew that this would be a friendship. He didn't make fun of me or question me. It seemed like he thought I was cool! I guess I fooled him.

In the same corner of the desk where Rehan's Quran sat, I placed my *Federal Income Taxation: A Law Student's Guide to the Leading Cases and Concepts*. Don't ask me why. I wanted to be as confident as Rehan, and just as distinguished.

"Bro, you better put that away," he warned.

"What?"

He spoke in a low whisper again. "Ms. Soraya ..."

"Huh?"

Just then, the mythological beast of math stepped into the room, and Rehan grabbed what I liked to call my *FIT* book (learning about taxes makes you fit) and dropped it into my bag. I guess a book about taxes was a more serious threat than a holy book.

———————————| MISFIT MOTIVATION |———————————

You will have horrible teachers. They're miserable because they're not paid enough and their spouses left them. Do your best in these situations.

HELL

"Ladies and gentlemen," Ms. Soraya pronounced in her ill-fitting black pants and floral tunic, smacking her hands together to silence us. Her lipstick was too pink, her eyeshadow was too blue, and I'm pretty sure she was wearing a wig. She reminded me of Tyler Perry's Madea.

Rehan leaned in. "Man, this shit gets scary. Just wait."

Ms. Soraya had a reputation. Rehan's face said it all. "Roll call!" she announced. *Attendance* might have been a more applicable word. "Susan?"

"Here," a cheery blonde replied.

"Matthew?" she asked in seeming fury.

"Here." He raised his hand, wearing a vintage AC/DC shirt. I'm pretty sure that was the guy who threw the cup at me.

"Rehan?"

"Yes, ma'am."

"Maryam?"

Time stood still. Purple-dress girl had finally been revealed in the seat forty-five degrees to the southeast.

"I'm here."

Against my better judgment, I let "يا إلهي" (the Arabic OMG) slip from my lips.

The magical Goddess Maryam turned her head, revealing her crystal-black eyes and supermodel-like features.

Even at this tender age, I knew that I was screwed. My desire to purchase a Lambo was now essential so that I might be the peacock displaying his gorgeous feathers to attract his mate.

————————— | MISFIT MOTIVATION | —————————

If you think the girl of your dreams is in the room, gently scan the perimeter. Do not do a spit take like I did on this occasion.

THE BEGINNING OF THE END

As the brown Angel of Allah—literally of any God for that matter—captivated my full attention, Ms. Soraya must have asked, "Hisham?"

I was lost in the beautiful oasis that was the back of Maryam's head.

"Hisham?"

Couldn't hear a thing. Totally gone …

"Hisham!"

Coming back to reality, I was instantly terrified and could not reply. As I reached for my backpack to grab my steno notepad and appear productive, the backpack ripped apart again. Fixing that zipper was clearly an innovation I hadn't mastered …

As my books, napkin ideas, and special "treasure box" spilled onto the floor, Ms. Soraya approached and clawed my items from the ground.

She looked down upon me like a cartoon villain, and I looked up at her as though Godzilla was tearing apart a skyscraper. Rehan placed his hands over his eyes.

"You never *attend* this class …"

"I … I … can still take the tests, though."

Monster Soraya proceeded to throw my belongings in the trash—tax book, *Rich Dad Poor Dad*, *The Outsider*—everything.

"Damn!" Rehan bemoaned.

I was happy for at least that much brotherhood, but truth be told, I was on the verge of tears.

Ms. Soraya might very well be the librarian's demonic twin sister. She placed her hands on her hips and admonished, "Hisham, this is a math class. The rest of this"—she motioned to the trash—"is bupkis!"

As I looked over to Rehan's sunken face, my courage came to the surface in a weird way. This new friend felt for me—truly felt for me—and so I was ready to do something I'd never imagined.

Get out of here, man, Rehan's warm expression pleaded.

———————— | MISFIT MOTIVATION | ————————

When it comes to making friends, it's chemistry, like anything else. True friends will give you the courage to do unimaginable things. Give back to them as much as they give to you, and if they silently advise you to bolt, then bolt.

GENIUS ESCAPE

I got up slowly from my desk, the back of my shirt still wet. I headed over to the cubbyholes where students kept their personal storage boxes. Well, I'd never had one because I didn't come to class enough. I managed to find an empty one with two sides ripped off and an ominous yellow stain on the bottom. I picked it up and willed myself not to smell it.

Remaining calm, I returned to the trash can that had become a dump truck for my very soul and pulled the items out one by one as the room went silent.

"What do you think you're doing, young man?" Soraya huffed like a fiery dragon.

Once everything was in the box and I'd held the tears and anger back long enough, I turned to Ms. Soraya. "I must go." It came out way too noble and 1800s, but I thought it might impress Maryam.

At my back, I heard the ملاك (Angel's) voice. "Hisham, you've left your backpack."

I turned to her, petrified but still responding with dignified silence while puffing out my chest. This John Wayne performance didn't last long as I struggled with the door handle and the box full of my life. I eventually pushed the door open with my hip. "Fuck."

Soraya remained in a permanent state of pissed. "Hisham?"

"Shit … I'm sorry."

I heard snickers from the class as I finally escaped the dungeon. My next destination was the nurse's office to get the seal of approval to leave. It was immensely awkward, holding the busted piece-of-crap box with the mysterious stain.

"Hisham, you're not feeling well?"

"No, ma'am. I feel like I'm gonna puke, and I have a cough." I added a fake cough for good measure.

"Let me check your temperature."

I thought of Maryam in an attempt to raise my body temperature. "I might faint."

The nurse looked at me in disbelief and heaved a sigh. "I'll call your father."

"Could you please tell him to meet me at STEM?"

She cocked her head to the side in confusion and looked at my awkward box. "Hisham, it looks like you just got fired from a job!"

"I fired myself, ma'am."

With that, she chuckled to herself and picked up the phone.

—————————————— | MISFIT MOTIVATION | ——————————————

Sometimes things get trashed. These experiences will continue to make you into a stronger person. Ultimately, being an innovator requires you to walk across the room and pull your shit out of the trash with everyone watching.

EXPRESSING THE PAIN

I was done with school. Done with everything.

Getting on the bus with your bike and a broken box of ambitions is not for the faint of heart. There were stares from the other passengers, but at that point, I was so numb that none of it mattered. STEM was my destination where I'd announce my retirement from any kind of labor or mental strain sixty years before that was even plausible.

As the bus bumped along, a charming grandma in a crocheted sweater asked, "Where are you going, young man?"

"Nowhere," I muttered.

Once I'd reached my stop, I traversed the center aisle with napkins spilling everywhere. I was convinced the box stain wasn't piss at this point because it smelled like Lysol.

Box in one hand, the pedals of my bike in the other (awkwardly pulling it down the steps), I dropped the Trek onto the sidewalk and approached the STEM warehouse. Passing the stunned lady at the front desk, I said, "Don't ask."

I went straight to Mr. Faizan's office. When I pulled open the door, he looked no less stunned by my disheveled entrance. This was when emotion no longer had to be held back. I dropped my box of failure onto his desk and said, "I don't deserve this anymore."

Mr. Faizan remained calm. "What do you mean, Hisham?"

My chin quivered. "I don't want to talk about it . . ." I said, letting the tears fall.

Mr. Faizan got up and stood in front of me. "Speak, if you can."

I barely could, but through the pain, the words began to fly. "I don't deserve to be treated this way. I don't deserve to be in math class. I feel like I can't solve a simple problem."

"That's far from the truth."

"I don't deserve to hold on to all this crap in my head." I pointed toward the box. "I don't even want to. It hurts a lot of the time. I don't deserve to be in STEM."

Mr. Faizan rifled through and pulled out my treasure chest—a catacomb for my special ideas that were probably shit too. I'd scribbled the word "Rival" with a Sharpie. "What does this mean?"

"I dunno—I just thought of it. The idea for a business or something." I felt so stupid even admitting to that, like a waste of time and waste of space with hidden ambition that should also be thrown in the trash.

"Can I go through all your stuff?" Mr. Faizan asked.

After one too many demands today, the answer was crying out "I don't care. I'm done."

| MISFIT MOTIVATION |

It doesn't matter what Misfit Mogul stage you're at:
you'll want to give up several times. Understand that
this is legit and we all go through it. In these moments,
take a breath and reassess, but do not give up.
These moments happen to teach you something.

THE "END" OF NAPKIN IDEAS

When my father met me outside, standing beside my tipped-over bicycle on the sidewalk, I tried to man up, but it was impossible.

"I'm sorry," I said.

"Are you actually sick?"

I shook my head. "I just didn't want to stay in school today."

"What did Mr. Faizan say?" he asked.

"I just gave him all my shit and ran—sorry." I quickly glanced up to gauge my dad's response. He held firm. "I don't deserve to be here. I'm not even smart. I just memorize things. Nobody likes me." Admitting this last bit was the moment of truth. "Someone … someone threw something at me."

He stepped in. "I'm sorry, son."

"It doesn't even matter." I nearly yelled as I picked up my sad Trek bike. "And …"—I wanted to say that I was in love, but Dad would kill me—"there's a very nice girl who witnessed my shame."

"Do I know her parents?"

I shook my head.

Dad gave me a stare that said a thousand words. "Then don't think of that." He placed a hand on my back and helped me put my bike in the car.

We drove home in silence, and I felt my first tinge of relief. I'd left school, left STEM, and discarded my napkin ideas and whatever else had been occupying my head like a Disney Imagineer on cocaine. This was it.

As the streets of Texas quickly passed by in Dad's Volvo, I decided to fully release my dreams. I'd move to Hawaii. Perhaps I'd sell ice cream on the beach and watch girls in bikinis, attend luaus, and eat SPAM … I would need to innovate the leis. Maybe there was a way to make them last forever without using plastic.

Pulling into the driveway and turning off the ignition, my father finally spoke. "You've reached ليل الروح المظلم at a young age." He used the Arabic words for the *dark night of the soul*.

I petulantly turned to him, needing his guidance more than ever. "What's the answer, then?"

"*Tomorrow*, son." He patted me on the shoulder. "Tomorrow."

——————————— | MISFIT MOTIVATION | ———————————

There's always tomorrow. If you felt like a shit show today, if the world was unkind and you stopped believing in yourself, wake up to a new day. Something is waiting for you on the other side

Winston Churchill once said, "Success is not final; failure is not fatal: it is the courage to continue that counts." I love this quote because it's important to realize that things will suck but they always change. I had a hard time growing up, and as my father shared, the *dark night of the soul* truly happens. There's so much emotion when it comes to being an Outsider. Perhaps you're teased or bullied, your stuff gets thrown into the trash, or quite frankly, you hate yourself and don't believe in the future. The truth is that you must keep going. We can fill our heads with phrases like "This too shall pass," or, "One day, it will all make sense," but these realizations don't help in the moment.

At this point in the story, I made an enduring friend who remains my closest today. I met a girl who captured my heart and imagination (and she still does today). Most importantly, Dreaming + Reality = *Confusion* reminds you that we're sometimes in more pain than we let on. You can have amazing ideas and still be the bird falling from the sky, often not by your own choosing.

In the next chapter, we talk about a different stage of this dark night of the soul. And as you go from an Outsider to a Misfit Mogul, you'll notice that the stages—and the potential—are infinite. Below is an example of the first stage of STEM: identifying a problem.

Invisible Homework

- What was the worst moment you had in school? It could be in the past or recently.

- There's a fundamental truth behind this moment: you received the key to your future success. Reflect on how a terrible incident in school might turn into a good thing. Someone threw soda at you, and you met a friend who stood up for you. The Old School will bring you down, but the Misfit rises up.

- I'm not gonna try to bore you with STEM stuff, but what it's all about is finding problems. A few examples the class is presented with include the following:

  1. *Walls cracking from water*

  2. *Blackouts from lightning*

  3. *White shorts turning yellow from stains (I kid you not)*

- In my Outsider life, the problems looked like this:

  1. *Hate school.*

  2. *Hate streetlamp.*

  3. *Maryam doesn't pay attention to me.*

- Below, write three small problems you see in the world and then three personal problems you're facing.

Notes 'n' Stuff:

3

THE MOMENT OF MOMENTS

The phoenix rises from the ashes

"Tomorrow," my father had said.

When *tomorrow* arrived, my eyes were burning red from all the crying the night before. Had I made a mistake? I'd given up on school, STEM, and all of my ideas. I'd basically given up on my life, and although the Hawaii idea was still unrealistic, I continued to consider it. Who needs a Lambo when you're a half-naked fire dancer covered in tattoos?

The plan was this: I'd come downstairs for breakfast and inform Dad that I was calling in sick again. There was no way I could face Ms. Soraya—or the librarian, for that matter—no way I could face the kids in the quad hurling soft drinks at me, and definitely no way I could face Maryam, even though I must have looked kind of cool yesterday with my painfully silent exit.

No, school was not happening, and my father and I had come to enough of an understanding in the last few days that he might understand. Even if he didn't, I'd behave like one of those dogs you see on viral videos who just lie there, refusing to move, their owner having to drag them across the parking lot.

Coming down the steps, I felt my breath catch in my chest. My father wouldn't like my plan for the day, despite his inspiring comment about *tomorrow*—a metaphor for how things could change—but I'd seen nothing change and didn't expect change on any given *tomorrow*.

What I saw in the kitchen came as a real shock. There wasn't just one newspaper in front of a face but two. Both papers came down at the same time, revealing Mr. Faizan at my father's side.

"Hisham," he said.

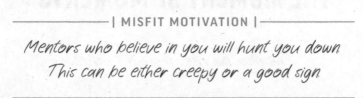

| MISFIT MOTIVATION |

Mentors who believe in you will hunt you down.
This can be either creepy or a good sign.

THE RED-EYED, BLOODY NOSE WONDER

I instantly felt a nosebleed and ran to the bathroom, mortified. Grasping the cold porcelain sink, I peered at myself in the mirror. Sure enough, my nose was bleeding out, and my eyes were bloodshot from the crying. There was no way of escaping my feelings; they were written all over my face. The knock on the door made me jump.

"Hisham, it's okay. We can talk."

"I'm, um …" I stalled, rolling a Kleenex into my nose to stop the bleeding. "I think my stomach hurts. Gonna be in here for a while." This lame excuse was probably worse than the truth, but I was buying myself time.

"Listen, if that's the case, I understand, but I'd like to speak with you when you're ready."

Sitting on the bathroom floor in defeat is not something I recommend, but I did it anyway. I clutched myself, turning into a sad little ball. There was no more chance of escape. If Mr. Faizan had come to my house, I guessed he actually cared.

I said, "Yeah, I was kinda lying. You can open the door."

"Okay." Once the door was open, Mr. Faizan took a deep breath. Pity, I assumed. "Are you all right?" He sat beside me, both our backs leaning against the tub.

"Do I *look* all right?" I let him inspect my eyes, the whites completely stained. "I look like a horror movie."

Mr. Faizan gravely replied, "I've seen some horror movies, and this isn't bad."

Just then, knowing that two large Kleenexes were stuck in each nostril finally cracked me up bad to the point of crying again. Mr. Faizan caught this contagion and started to laugh too. I pointed to my tissue-stuffed nose. "This is ridiculous."

"Listen." He got up, grabbed two tissues, and stuck them in his nose. "If solidarity helps you to talk, I can do this all day."

=| MISFIT MOTIVATION |=

There will be people who show up for you It's okay to be vulnerable with them In fact, it opens a door.

RETURN TO THE INFERNO

Mr. Faizan drove me to school and said, "I'll see you at STEM in the afternoon."

I looked out the window of his car in loathing. "You have no idea how painful this will be."

"I do, actually. It was the same for me."

Pushing my head back into the passenger seat's headrest in agony, I clutched the new box that Mr. Faizan had given me with all my belongings restored to yesterday's standards. Ah, with all my father's talk of *tomorrow*, why wasn't there any great discussion about *yesterday*?

I noticed one thing missing—my Rival box. I turned to Mr. Faizan and asked, "Bro, you keeping my stuff?"

He grinned. "First of all, my name isn't *Bro*, and secondly, I'm keeping it temporarily for a reason."

"To steal my shit," I joked.

"No ... to make something of it. Go on now."

I glared at Mr. Faizan as though he were a shepherd leading me into a lion's den. The nosebleed had subsided, but my eyes were still red. It always lasted for days—my visible little-kid status was on full display for all to see.

"Hisham," he said through the rolled-down window. "It will be fine."

I flipped Mr. Faizan the bird before he drove off. The gesture wasn't intentionally mean; it meant I was beginning to trust him.

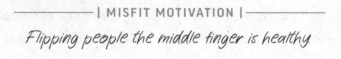

| MISFIT MOTIVATION |

Flipping people the middle finger is healthy.

THE PHOENIX STILL IN THE ASHES

The slow and painful walk to Ms. Soraya's class while clutching a cardboard box for the second day in a row felt like walking through mud. I remembered the nurse's statement about how it looked like I just lost a job when I fled school the day before. Now, I was that pathetic employee returning with their tail between their legs.

I was one minute late to math, so you can imagine the slow and painful walk from the doorway to my desk. I couldn't bear to look at Maryam (but I noted the pretty white hijab in my peripheral vision). Dropping my box on the desk, I felt Rehan lean over.

"Savage."

I shook my head. There was nothing savage about making a huge life decision one day and going back on your plan the next day. (If I needed five personalities to impress Maryam before, now I needed one hundred.)

Ms. Soraya eyed me with the cringe of someone smelling fish. "Well, then ... everyone turn to page sixty-nine."

Aha! Two auspicious numbers combined. Maybe it would be a better day ... Rifling through my brand spanking new cardboard box, I discovered the math book was nowhere to be found. *Shitttttttttt!* Had I even brought it the day before? Surely Soraya from Hell wouldn't have thrown the math book in the trash. But she was so twisted, there was a chance ...

Ms. Demon started scribbling numbers on the chalkboard, and I was yet again ready to run to the nurse's office. Mr. Faizan was a liar! I'd bust his balls later. *It will be fine*, he'd said. Something was seriously wrong with that guy.

All hope was lost until I heard Rehan's desk slide into mine. He opened his math book and shared it with me. My heart skipped a beat. He sensed my 7.0 earthquake panic and came in to help. Rehan gently put out his fist again (like a fist bump whisper), and I met his with mine.

—————————— | MISFIT MOTIVATION | ——————————

Returning to a place of pain and obscurity can be helpful. The hope for a better **tomorrow** *keeps us going. Leaning into tomorrow after a bad yesterday is a win.*

THE DIAMOND IN THE ROUGH ... OF DESPAIR

I stared transfixed at the back of Maryam's head the whole class, my chin resting in my hand. From the shape, it looked like her hair was in a bun, and I imagined her taking off her hijab and unlocking her hair for me to see. I was pretty much screwed.

"Hisham!" Ms. Soraya clapped her hands to wake me up from my paradisal dream.

"Yes, ma'am," I replied, quickly looking over at Rehan's book to pretend like I was intently focused on the lesson.

She pointed her finger to a complex math problem poorly written on the board. "Answer this!"

"Oh, okay." My boredom was apparent. "That's 56.97."

Ms. Soraya stepped back and pointed to another problem.

"That's 219.01."

She appeared flummoxed by this fast response as she reached for her bottle of Diet Coke to assuage her confusion. I returned my attention to the back of Maryam's head. The Angel turned to me, and I caught her black eyes, sensing a tinge of admiration. All the other girls snickered, and Rehan brought a celebratory admonishment. "Dude, stay focused."

My gaze remained fixed on the only beautiful thing in this horrible room. "I *am* focused, bro."

The school bell rang, and I could have collapsed in relief. Still, there was Tupperware dread. To my amazement, Maryam met me in the hall, carrying my broken backpack.

"I have this for you," Allah's Angel of diamond-like, euphoric beauty said.

"I …" My inner James Bond disappeared when I needed him most. "Um, cool. But keep it."

She tilted her phenomenal head to the side. "Why?"

The floodgates exploded. *Don't do it, man*, I thought to myself.

"The construction is bad. I've come up with a new idea for how to get the zipper not to break, and even that invention has not worked. Ultimately, I think the design is faulty, and the logo could be improved as well. There's something about the color scheme that isn't quite right. Also, the straps aren't exactly ergonomically sound, and that needs improvement as well. I'd take it back merely as a lab experiment, but I think there's a poor balance of form and function."

Oops.

Maryam lifted her luscious eyebrow and walked away in confusion.

─────── | MISFIT MOTIVATION | ───────

You'll be hearing more about my floodgates When you're a geek, this is the apparatus by which verbal vomit comes out about something cool and innovative but can't seem to talk in real life

TUPPERWARE TALES

That lunch period was unlike any other. Finally, I was seated on the cold cement bench with an actual table in front of me and a real-life human beside me. Rehan and I pulled out our Tupperware simultaneously.

"What did you get, bro?" Rehan asked.

I cringed when I replied, "Two-day-old samosa."

Rehan threw his head back in shame. "That is rough!"

Although it was comforting to have a companion, my familiar introverted panic reared its head. "What … um, what do you have?"

"Halal club sandwich."

I wasn't going to let this go. I had to comment. "Dude, that is so Muslim-American bougie."

Rehan shrugged. "Better than an old samosa."

Fair point.

We sat and examined the quad as we ate our lunches, like two old men sitting on a porch.

He brought up a sensitive topic. "Yesterday was rough, dude."

I choked on my dry lunch and reached for my box of fruit juice. "Yeah, it wasn't cool," I managed to reply.

"You gonna keep coming back to school?"

"I guess so."

"You're so smart! Like, you just looked up and had the answers to those math questions. If I were you, I'd just leave school and do something better."

My new friend made a great point. I wanted to leave more than anything. This stirred the most romantic statement I'd ever made in my young life: "My true love is here."

"Bro, it's too soon to be calling me that."

My cheeks flushed as I keeled over in laughter. "Dude ... no!" I waved my hands in the air, unable to speak as the humor knocked the wind out of me. "Maryam, dude. Maryam!"

Rehan shook his head. "No personality."

"She's so pretty!"

The Mountain Dew villain in the tank top (they were all dudes in tank tops at this point) approached our table carrying his cup of soda. My hair stood on end. Would this happen again? And in front of my only friend?

Rehan stood to his full height, just as tall as the asshole bully. "Not today, الأحمق (*asshole*)." After those words, the jock walked away, not knowing that he'd been called an asshole. "Bro," Rehan said after victoriously seating himself.

"Bro."

Finding like-minded people who support you is rare, but when you find it, don't let go. I remain best friends with Rehan to this day. I stand up for him, and he stands up for me. Never let go of this kind of bond.

THE MOMENT

"Sit down, Hisham," Mr. Faizan said, watching me as I crossed his office and sat in an industrial chair. "How did it go today at school?"

"It was … better, I guess." This was hard to admit. My father's notion of *tomorrow* and my dread of *yesterday* had proved my dad to be right. But what the hell would the next tomorrow look like?

"I'm glad to hear it."

I noticed my Rival box on his desk. "Why did you keep this?"

"Because I have an idea for you."

I could use all the help I could get. "What idea?"

Mr. Faizan pulled open a drawer and pushed a piece of paper across the table. "I want to help you form your first company."

Spiritually, my chair flipped over backward, but in reality, I was still sitting in stunned silence. I couldn't help but respond, "Um, cool?"

He resurrected my notes from the Rival box, placing them neatly in front of me. "What you have here are innovations that can work. I see it clearly." He pointed to each one. "The apparel, the lamp, kitchen appliances, technology, furniture."

I felt exposed. These ideas came out due to a spinning mind. It seemed preposterous to turn them into reality. I was just blowing steam as I saw problems everywhere. When people ignore you, you escape into something else—you travel from the tangible world to your idea of how the world *could* be. Its potential.

"I want to help you, Hisham. I know about innovation and business; your father knows about finance. I already own a company worth twenty-five million dollars."

I had to tease him. "Not very impressive."

Mr. Faizan laughed as I recalled how he was on my bathroom floor that morning with tissues stuck up his nose. "You can do better than me," he imparted. "Your father and I have spoken on the phone several times, and we both agree. You can do better than us *all*."

This nonreality was hard to accept. I was still a lanky kid with no friends (except for one!), and I felt like an utter mess in every respect. My knock-off Ralph Lauren polo shirt was the only thing that made me look respectable. And even that had a stain …

I asked, "Why should I push harder? I know a lot, but nothing makes sense!"

Mr. Faizan's eyes twisted to the side in a pensive haze. The light outside the window went brighter, cueing his words with harmonic brightness. "Because there's more to life than what you're experiencing now. You're suffering, and I know it all too well. You're alone—the Outsider, the Misfit. The kid who doesn't fit in. But what I see in your sketches is something that no one else has imagined, and these ideas need to be approached quickly. Your *Old School* is terrible, yes, but I'm providing you with a *New School*, a place where you're taught inspiration before all the rest."

This was getting very teacher-like, and I recoiled. "Still, man, I don't know *why* I should make more effort. It means nothing!"

"To save you from yourself."

My chest constricted. The humor was evident as my nosebleed rapidly returned. "How am I supposed to do that?" I asked, reaching for a handful of my shirt to stop the deluge of blood.

Mr. Faizan stopped my hand and offered me a tissue instead.

"By setting yourself free. Setting up your future. Believing in your ideas. Come under my wing. Let me help you. I'm here for you."

"Why?"

"I want to make you the man you're destined to become."

As I dabbed my nose, the bloody wellspring of anxiety and loneliness, one thought came to mind: *No one has ever said these things to me before.*

| MISFIT MOTIVATION |

If you're persistent, you always have "that moment" —the moment of moments. It's the moment when someone believes in you, and more importantly, you catch a glimmer of believing in yourself. It's an open door within. It's the moment when you see your potential and latch on to that vision.

The *phoenix rises from the ashes* in a singular moment, followed by several other moments. There are signs. People around you support the ascension. It's important to realize that before this happens, you dip into the flames. That turmoil is not only okay, but it's also important. We have to have the most difficult moments before we rise. I saw a new opportunity when I joined the STEM school, but that was only the beginning. I still carried the fears and rejection.

Fortitude. Fortitude might not even be the right word. *Vulner-ability.* Most of the Moguls of our world have taken tough hits—they've been Outsiders and Misfits—and none of this deters success. Fully be who you are in this moment and trust that your bloody nose, red crying eyes, and general discomfort will never hold you back. There's sincere discomfort at our age, but that's awesome. It's not fun, but if you're in discomfort, it can transform you into something great.

The *moment of moments* will happen for you if you find the right people and stick to your guns (still hate that phrase). You're dreaming about something or perhaps a thousand things. These ideas might get thrown in the trash, but pull them out and act like John Wayne with the pretty girl who wants to save your backpack. "James Bond" this situation within your amazing, awkward self. Do it because it's necessary. For the time being ...

And I sincerely apologize for what's below because I want you to see what it looks like. Don't hate me.

Invisible Homework

- Simple: Write down all the people who make you feel good about yourself. They boost your confidence. Now, write down the names that don't (fuckers).

- In chapter 2, you wrote down some serious problems. In STEM, we do something called starbursting[3] to solve them. Starbursting is a form of brainstorming that focuses on generating questions rather than answers, but I'd rather you just get a pack of Starbursts and save me the yellow ones. Really, all it is is asking questions about your top problems. I'll give you the streetlamp analysis because the Maryam thing was too hard on my youthful heart.

- Streetlamp Questions:

  1. *Why did they decide to make it so bright?*

  2. *What light bulb are they using?*

  3. *Why did my dad position me in this room so that it shines through my window?*

  4. *Who benefits from that lamp?*

  5. *Why is it up so high?*

  6. *How much do taxpayers dish out for that thing?*

  7. *Is it energy efficient?*

- You get the idea. Now, start asking questions about one of your problems that you listed previously.

---

3 MasterClass, 2022, https://www.masterclass.com/articles/starbursting.

Notes 'n' Stuff:

4

PROBLEM AFTER PROBLEM

Life dishes out lemons.
The Misfit Mogul makes lemonade

Mr. Faizan pulled the cap from his marker and wrote on the white-board in bold letters, *Porch Piracy*. He scanned the STEM warehouse room and asked, "Do you know what that is?"

Mikhail raised his hand. "When they steal your shit."

The class snickered, but I thought it was a legit answer. Even Mr. Faizan had to grin. "That's true, Mikhail. It's when people steal your *stuff*. It's a very common problem that is getting worse. And what's our lesson for today? Solving problems in a new way ..."

My inner nerd got pretty excited and frustrated at the same time. I already had the answer and could sketch it if I got bored long enough. I took a deep breath, turned to Alexis (who was staring at me), and let the NASA maestro continue. If I could have given him a conductor's baton, I would have.

"I want each of you to come up with ten reasons for this problem."

Reasons for the problem? It seemed simple, and Mikhail had said it eloquently: people are going to steal your shit when you're not at home. Even though this exercise seemed tedious, I took out my steno pad, which was definitely crazy-librarian approved, and wrote down some thoughts:

1. People buy too much shit on Amazon

2. No one was home

3. Your ex-husband or ex-wife knows where you live

4. Super easy to steal It's a cardboard box

5. Your neighbors hate you

6. The UPS guy shook the box and knew something good was in there

7. Your Ring camera doesn't work

8. The pirate wore a hoody it said Ring camera did work

9. You were stupid enough to order before going on vacation

10. A bear took it

I was feeling confident with my list as Mr. Faizan proceeded. "Now, what are ten solutions for this problem, based on the variables that you wrote down?"

My pen went to work for me, gliding along the steno gracefully on autopilot:

1. Buy shit in stores

2. Don't leave your house

3. Do not disclose to your ex where you live

4. Create a lockbox (This one had potential)

5. Don't be mean to your neighbors

6. Become friends with your UPS guy

7. Fix the Ring camera

8. Ban hoodies for those with criminal records

9. *Order when you return from vacation*

10. *Let the bear have it. Move on with your life ...*

After this next brainstorming session, the students looked from side to side, gauging one another. There was genuine confusion in Mikhail's eyes, and some other kid just shook his head in dismay.

Mr. Faizan pointed to me. "Hisham?"

I eloquently responded, "Huh?"

"What solutions came to mind? I know that you have some." He leaned back on his desk and posed like a brown Richard Gere.

"Def have an idea," I replied. "Number four.

─────────────── | MISFIT MOTIVATION | ───────────────

*Solving problems comes down to surveying the problem from all angles. **Why** is it a problem? What are the various solutions that come to mind? With each solution, seek out more problems within the solution. This is how the human mind finds the ultimate recipe for lemonade*

───

SIMPLE SOLUTIONS

STEM was starting to feel like math class but without the Soraya of موت (Death) and the Maryam of جَنّة (Heaven). I knew the answer but wanted to play it off so no one would be annoyed with me. Sadly, the floodgates still managed to open.

"Mr. Faizan, I feel as though there are several factors that contribute to this problem. First of all, most people go to work five days a week and can't monitor their packages. Those who do have Ring cameras aren't protected. Pirates will wear hoodies to conceal their faces, and any inquiry with the police for a fifty-dollar purchase is not a priority. Also, our society is lacking in moral fortitude due to the current inflation and political unrest. There's increased theft throughout the country, and this can be attributed to the demise of the American soul. There are also bears."

"And?"

I sat in silence, knowing Mikhail would never be my friend, and even Alexis might not have a crush on me anymore. "But you just need a lockbox."

Mr. Faizan broke through the unbearable silence by asking, "What kind of lockbox?"

The whole thing had already been designed in my brain, so I explained further. "Just a box that remains open, and when UPS or Amazon comes, they place the package in the lockbox and seal it. The homeowner will have a code to unlock it."

"What size?"

"It should be quite large. People order everything these days. Although I don't imagine a pirate stealing an IKEA couch."

The class laughed, and I felt momentarily relieved. It was the most I'd spoken in STEM, and for whatever reason, talking about innovation allowed me to speak. This quickly came to an end as I felt all eyes on me with Mr. Faizan's statement, "Pirates do steal IKEA couches."

"Yes ... yes, sir." I doodled on my steno. "I've heard it reported. In the news ... and in ... several magazines."

For whatever reason, my confidence was quickly lost. I could see the innovation in my head: the lockbox, an aesthetic design that made it look charming on the porch (flower design for women, football logos for men), the end to porch pirating, and an amazing invention that could change the world! But how the hell was that gonna happen?

----- | MISFIT MOTIVATION | -----

*You can come up with a million solutions in your head,
but that's just the beginning. Your napkin ideas have
incredible potential, but you must keep asking the
right questions to create a true innovation. If indeed
a bear is the legitimate problem, just let it go, man.*

COMPLEX SOLUTIONS

Alexis (a.k.a., girl with patent) chimed in. "I think that homes should have a special door. You know, like a doggie door, and the UPS person pushes the package inside."

I was rolling my eyes internally but concealed my frustration.

Mr. Faizan was quick to speak. "Let's consider Alexis's plan." He wrote on the whiteboard, *Find the gaps. What could go wrong?*

I could picture a hundred different gaps in this weak plan, but I wrote down five:

1. *Pirate sneaks into doggy door.*

2. *Baby bear sneaks into doggy door.*

3. *Dog is pissed because it's not his door.*

4. *UPS guy comes into your house and steals stuff.*

5. *Ring camera just laughs at you.*

After writing down these ideas, I kept to myself until Mr. Faizan asked, "Hisham, what did you discover in your notes?"

Fumbling, I took one look into Alexis's anticipating eyes and replied, "I think it's a good plan but has a few flaws." I was being gentle …

"What flaws do you see?"

Floodgates broke again. "The delivery person would need to lock the door. Otherwise, that would leave the house insecure for the entire day while the person is away. Ultimately, this creates an even greater threat of theft. Mosquitoes can come through small cracks in anything. Flies and bees could do the same. It's a huge price to pay after you've already dropped some cash for your Amazon earbuds that could have been purchased at a drugstore."

"So what would you propose, Hisham?"

"How much time do you have?"

MINDFUCK SOLUTIONS

"I have all the time in the world, Dr. Watson."

Faizan called my bluff. "Sherlock Holmes, sketch your lockbox idea on the board."

It was a moment of sheer terror. Sitting in *any* classroom with Soraya-induced PTSD was scary enough, constantly pondering the thoughts of others and lost in my own mind. To make matters worse, I now contemplated these harsh lights overhead, the table that was too tall, and the vending machine that you had to kick to get your Snickers bar. Still, I persevered, standing from my rickety stool and wishing that I had an exoskeleton to carry me through my fatigue.

My hand had a visible tremor as I sketched the design. I added dimensions, turned to the STEM class, and spoke in a late-night infomercial tone. "The box would remain open, and the delivery person would seal it when the packages arrive. The consumer would simply use a passcode to open it."

Mr. Faizan pressed on. "And how would the lockbox not be stolen?"

"It could be … screwed into the wall."

"And how could the pirate not *unscrew* it?"

My mind was going in a million different directions as this talk of screwing was getting to me. "It could be incredibly heavy."

"But *multiple* pirates could pick it up."

Mikhail raised his hand. "It could be charged like an electrical fence."

Mr. Faizan laughed. "Then the UPS man would be electrocuted."

Mikhail realized his error and frowned.

I had my two cents to add. "Theft is largely psychological. If the perpetrator sees a heavy box, they'd rather go to the neighbor's house. They'd go to a property owned by someone who doesn't possess this product because they're looking for what's easy."

Mr. Faizan nodded in approval. "And if everyone has one of these boxes, what then?"

This dude was getting on my last nerve. It was a solid point, but he had me down the rabbit hole. "Robbers will turn to robbing banks again, like the good old days."

My mentor's face fell.

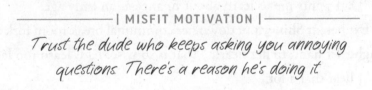

—————— | MISFIT MOTIVATION | ——————

Trust the dude who keeps asking you annoying questions. There's a reason he's doing it.

TIME FOR A BREAK

Being an "apprentice" at my father's accounting firm after STEM made the days long, but it was either that or video games. And Master Kiyosaki's passage had me curious. Brace yourself:

"The tax man will take as much as you let him. The tax system is ultimately fair in that it works the same for everyone who has the same situation. If you are willing to invest, the tax laws will work in your favor. If you want to just spend money and buy liabilities, the tax laws won't give you any breaks—and it's likely you will pay the whole tax possible."[4]

This incomprehensible knowledge had me sitting in the break room awkwardly staring at a woman by the name of Shirley. She ate a Lean Cuisine as I stared at my Tupperware of cold haleem. "You seem like a nice young man," she said with a smile.

My reply was so pathetic that I still can't believe it. "I am, thank you."

Shirley took a forkful of her microwaved dish and added, "Your father brought you here to learn about finance?"

"Yes, ma'am."

"How wonderful!" She clapped her hands together, then pinched my cheek. "There's so much to learn." Leaning in, Shirley whispered with a giggle, "Especially for a kid like *you*."

This was a confusing *inflection*. Up until this point, I was only a Misfit in my own mind (Dad could sense it, I guess), but an Outsider at heart. Truth be told, I wanted to be a Misfit in my daily actions, but that would require moving out of my family home.

"Dad wants me to learn about finance at an early age."

Exuberant Shirley put down her communal break room fork and brought her hand to her heart. "That is so wise. Kids learn too late."

"I hear that a lot."

"Do you want to be a CPA, like your dad? My goodness, he's so talented and impressive!"

I had to consider this question for a moment. Yeah, my dad was successful, but something was missing. An image flashed through my mind: the moment he saw my copy of *Rich Dad Poor Dad* and grew

---

4   Kiyosaki, *Rich Dad Poor Dad*.

nostalgic. Nostalgic for the possibilities? The future? Whatever it was, something was missing for him and for me.

"I want to be an inventor," I proclaimed, then instantly felt stupid.

"Ooooh!" she cooed. Her excitement basically meant she'd just taken on the role of my adoptive الجدة (grandma). "What do you want to invent?"

As other coworkers entered the break room and my haleem still sat in front of me (I was afraid to put it in the microwave for the same reasons previously described), I answered Shirley with great conviction, "Everything." It was as though the ghost of Mr. Faizan came tapping on my shoulder and whispered into my ear, "Say more, Hisham. What do you want to invent?"

Damn it. Let the adult-voiced shit show begin. "I'd like to make innovations that solve real-world problems. Today I came up with an idea for solving porch theft. I think it will make millions … or I don't know how much."

Shirley sat resolute and inspired. "Well, I need something like that for when I order my yarn." Her eyes grew misty. "And I'd be more than proud to do your taxes."

——————— | MISFIT MOTIVATION | ———————

Find your Shirley in life, bro. Find your Shirley…

TALES OF SHIRLEY AND THE GANG

I kept returning to my dad's CPA office to hang out with Shirley. Our lunch gatherings grew as accountants Mohammad, Omar, and Ralph joined the festivities. I had found my tribe. The aroma in the break room from Mohammad's Tupperware namkeen gosht (spicy lamb) made me feel seen and instilled in me the courage to heat my dish in the microwave.

Although I just wanted to hang with my new friends, Shirley insisted that I read aloud from *Federal Income Taxation: A Law Student's Guide to the Leading Cases and Concepts*. I seriously didn't want to, but I had to please Shirley. After all, she knitted her own sweaters, and I was impressed by that skill. I didn't have the heart to tell her I'd already read the whole book while other kids my age were at the movies.

As my voice cracked, I reasoned with myself that this was a practice in speaking, and since I felt safe with my adult friends, I didn't pause to panic. The customary responses also gave me fortitude. I read a dull passage, and Mohammad chimed in, "Bullshit. Bullshit. No true." He swiped his finger from left to right like a clock pendulum. "This book crap."

I loved his candor, but it was Omar who consistently provided the most winning rebuttals. "This book very good." He shrugged at Mohammad. "*You* crap. Terrible accountant."

They glared at one another as Ralph unleashed his floodgates of relatable nerdiness. "Gentlemen, I'd beg to differ. Chirelstein's seminal work is nothing short of genius. I've found that it mirrors many casebooks and allows a shorthand for a young man like Hisham to learn the basics of our trade. I return to this book most nights to sharpen my mind for the next day. One must practice the art of tax law each and every day."

Ralph's epic responses were not uncommon, but this time, even Shirley sat in shock, her sandwich dangling from her hand. Ralph was a bona fide Outsider, and I loved every time his freak flag flew. I mean … he was married, so someone must have liked his brain. In my mind, I was designing a mysterious pocket watch that only *serious* Outsiders could carry.

Shirley dropped her sandwich and reached over to take my hand. "Hisham, don't listen to these fools. This is what accounting does to the brain."

---------------- | MISFIT MOTIVATION | ----------------

Although accounting will cause any person to go insane, learn it anyhow. There are several old rich guys who barely pay taxes because they have read Federal Income Taxation: A Law Student's Guide to the Leading Cases and Concepts. They are not breaking the law; they merely understand the loopholes. They are ballers in their own right.

CPA MIGRAINE

As I walked into my father's office, I realized that there were only two places I ever found him—in an office of some sort or behind a newspaper at the breakfast table. He clicked away at the keyboard, an ornate Turkish tea set at the ready. Dad reached for his pillbox and took out two migraine tablets before swallowing them down with his Paki tea.

"Is that you, Hisham?" he asked, not taking his eyes off the screen.

"Yes, sir."

"Did you learn more today?"

I paused, wanting to share that Mohammad saying the word *crap* over and over again was the greatest lesson.

"I learned ... very much."

"Good, you need to know," he said, turning his chair away from the screen. "This information is vital and must be ascertained soon."

I couldn't help but ask, "Why is that?"

After removing his glasses, he swiped his eyes and took another sip of tea. "Mr. Faizan has told me of your invention. He says that it is marketable. It has a future."

"Cool," I replied blankly. "So, I just sell it to someone and make a lot of money?"

My father shook his head. "Hisham, I've seen changes in you since joining STEM, but this is just the beginning. Many things must fall into place. Make the design perfect, gain a patent, and continue to learn about finances."

This seemed so over the top and beyond me that the nosebleed instantly came. I rushed for a napkin in my pocket on which I'd drawn an idea for Shirley's next sweater design. "Yes, sir." The prospect of actually making my porch box into something real instantly terrified me. I loved to draw and invent, but the rest of the process? I just wanted to have my dad take care of it.

"Now, go off and study, son."

"G'day, sir." The fake British accent caused me to flee, but I stopped after rushing to the door. "I'm afraid I'll screw all this up …" I shared, dabbing my nose and petrified for the future.

He gave the *father sigh*, a mixture of frustration and understanding. After pulling out his copy of *Rich Dad Poor Dad*, dog-eared as much as the Quran, Dad read aloud, "School has conditioned us to avoid mistakes—and punishes students for making them. In the real world, I've learned that mistakes—if acknowledged and evaluated and used as a tool to make better decisions in the future—are invaluable."[5]

I stepped in and asked, "So I should … ?"

"Screw it up a hundred times, son."

—————————— | MISFIT MOTIVATION | ——————————

Kids are terrified of making mistakes, but fuckups are the keys to our futures. When it comes to innovations, you will make hundreds of mistakes, and that's part of the process. Shit show errors lead you to the game-changer lemonade.

---

5   Kiyosaki, *Rich Dad Poor Dad*.

THE PLAYDATE OF BRO

The first time Rehan came to my house to hang out, it was the most awkward experience of my life. The idea was suggested in the form of Rehan leaning over in math class saying, "Bro, we should chill sometime."

"Cool." I'd nodded in a daze. No friends had been over to my house before because it was the hallowed ground where only Ahmads could dwell with their shoes off.

When I opened the door to greet my new friend, the conversation sounded like this:

"Bro," Rehan greeted me.

"Bro," I replied.

He stepped inside. "Cool house, bro."

"Thanks, bro."

The primal language served a purpose. Having my first "playdate" as a teenager was fraught with mystery and discomfort. "We should chill now …" Rehan cleared his throat. "Like we talked about."

This uncomfortable beginning quickly changed once Rehan had my Nintendo controller in his hand, and then like magic, we'd known each other all our lives. He momentarily glanced at my lockbox sketch and remarked, "Dude, that looks bomb. It's a good idea."

"Mr. Faizan says I should patent it."

"What the heck is that?"

"Like, when you certify that it's unique, and you own the idea."

Rehan snickered. "Then you'd be like a millionaire? Maryam is gonna get all hot and bothered."

That was essentially the point, and even though my dad and the local Paki matchmaker would kill me, I responded, "Yes."

Rehan failed at *Mario Kart* and dropped the controller in dismay. He leaned back into my overstuffed beanbag with a piquant air of failure. "Give me a sec."

I was embarrassed for him. "Take your time."

He turned back to the sketch that I continued to evaluate, feeling my future on the line and my father's waning approval.

"How that thing work, man?"

"Bro, the delivery guy puts shit in there, and then the lid closes, and you use a code to open it."

"Huh." Rehan nodded in approval. "That's cool. My dad had a car part stolen once."

"Never again!" I said with that out-of-the-blue conviction of a late-night QVC salesman.

Rehan stared off into the distance as though Allah were speaking to him. "Bro, what if a squirrel gets trapped in there or some shit?"

This moment of moments helped Mr. Faizan's advice to finally sink in: keep investigating the problems till you reach the ultimate solution.

The *answer* to this problem came swiftly. It was the smartest thing Rehan had ever said to me.

———————————— | MISFIT MOTIVATION | ————————————

Listen to your stupid friend. He knows something...
*(Just playing: Rehan is rad) But **do** listen to your*
friends and mentors. One mind cannot find the
best solution to a problem. Many minds do.

Making lemonade from lemons is a common phrase, but that's what innovators do. We're constantly looking for ways to make something better. The process of doing this involves what Mr. Faizan taught me—continuously asking questions, finding solutions, and then questioning those solutions. Although my porch piracy invention was a success (why are those pirate assholes doing that?), it required the minds of others to bring it to perfection and even then ... I see the flaws.

Constantly learning and growing can seem exhausting at times. You already have homework and tons of random shit to learn, but push yourself to go further. At our age, that often requires finding adults who push *you*. Learning about finances was boring as hell, but Shirley, Mohammad, Omar, and Ralph made it easier. Seek out friendships with adults and learn from them. If they use the word *crap* a lot, you're quite lucky.

As the journey of the Misfit Mogul continues, be prepared for a migraine or a nosebleed because this stuff isn't easy, but it's setting up your future. Ultimately, the pivotal skill is talking to people—getting out of your shell and learning from others. Shirley helped me to do this (she made me a sweater too), but the real win was that I was acquiring skills that the Old School would never teach me. I'd reached my New School: practical knowledge and *people*. One day, I'd discover how to converse with them without sounding like an alien. This phenomenon comes many chapters from now. Till then, I'm gonna make you resent me once more:

Invisible Homework

With that one special problem you selected (yes, it can be a girl problem), work on a problem statement so that you can bore the shit out of *yourself*. Contextualize the problem (that streetlamp is in a bougie neighborhood where people ride their bikes at night like all freaks do), then state why the problem matters (I can't sleep, FFS), and then proclaim your aim for your work on this problem (to be able to see the stars better and stop obsessing).

- Write down a few brief notes for your problem statement.

    1. *Contextualize it.*

    2. *Why is the problem important?*

    3. *What's your aim when working on it?*

If you don't feel like doing this, just doodle things.

Notes 'n' Stuff:

PART II

THE
Innovator
MINDSET

5

SOLUTION AFTER SOLUTION

The Misfit Mogul has trouble sleeping

I was in bed tossing and turning with existential diarrhea as I dreamt of a squirrel trapped in my lockbox invention. The squirrel was crying out to me, "Hisham! Why did you invent this horrible box?"

"I'm so sorry, bro!" I moaned.

"I can't get to my nuts!"

This was a cheap joke on the imaginary squirrel's part, but I gave him props.

Instantly sitting up and looking at the bright streetlamp, I reasoned that the squirrel and Rehan had a valid argument for why the innovation didn't work. If the lockbox had a weight sensor and suddenly closed, anything could get in there and be trapped while someone was at work or on holiday, which were the two key problems that led to the need for this innovation in the first place. I swiped my hand across my sweaty brow.

I quickly raced downstairs, ready to careen through my busy day. "Good morning, Dad," I said, shoving my lunch Tupperware into my backpack.

The ominous newspaper was lowered. "You're in a hurry this morning."

His observation was just. My eyes were red (not from crying but from lack of sleep), and tremors in my body had kept waking me up throughout the night. It was no doubt the desperate squirrel jolting my nervous system ...

"I am in a hurry."

"Why, son?"

"There's a lot to do today."

The newspaper floated back up. "Do your best."

I wanted to scream but took this sentiment with a grain of salt. I had school and STEM, and then at the end of the day, I'd meet with Shirley and the gang. It was a stretch, but nice to be busy and distract myself from Misfit thoughts and Outsider feelings.

—————— | MISFIT MOTIVATION | ——————

If your thoughts are keeping you up at night, you're not alone. Constantly investigating any problem for the right solution is an ongoing effort and takes you down the rabbit hole. This insomniac focus is what your invention requires. But seriously, bro, try to get some sleep.

SORAYA GODZILLA

My math teacher sneered at me with a level of disgust that had no meaning or purpose. I'd shifted the situation in my mind, and the answer was clear: there was no doubt that Ms. Soraya hated me so much because she thought I was amazing.

The only one whom I truly wanted the loving death stare from was seated in front of me. Maryam wore a yellow dress and tan-colored hijab that day. She was a beacon of sunshine who did not once shine her light on my face. Starved of vitamin D, I turned toward Rehan, awkwardly pointing at Maryam's back and then creating a heart with my two folded hands. Rehan shook his head, no question doubting my capabilities. I would prove him wrong …

"Hisham!" Soraya Godzilla snapped.

"Yes, ma'am?"

"You didn't attend class yesterday …" She sat at her desk and angrily sipped a Frappuccino from a Christmas tumbler, way too ahead of the season.

I managed to supply my fake cough that no one believed anymore. "I was sick."

"Now that you've *started* to come to class, don't mess it up," she scolded.

The truth behind yesterday's ditch was hard to explain. I learned more from Shirley and the gang than I did in this nightmare. Perhaps the only benefit that math class provided was the opportunity to stare at the back of Maryam's head.

Soraya rose and proclaimed, "Class, I will now deliver your test scores."

Rehan shook in his seat like the squirrel in my dream. For my part, I didn't feel one ounce of fear. To be honest, I simply didn't care. Math class was more like *The Hunger Games* than a place of learning. I'd fare better with a sword than a math book.

"Maryam," Soraya announced, dropping the Angel's graded test on her desk.

I peered over Maryam's gorgeous shoulder and witnessed the ominous B-. If that were my score, Dad would kill me.

Soraya continued her promenade around the room. "Ali." She released his test like a heavy anvil. "Hamza." That test shook the desk like an earthquake. "Istanbul."

I just shook my head. How there were so many brown kids at this school, I couldn't understand. Why one was named Istanbul was even more confusing.

"Hisham," she announced, looking at me with that deep love and confusion that she no doubt felt. The test landed like a feather, and my status as Mr. Darcy was confirmed. When I saw the A+, everything came into focus: there was no reason to return to math class ever again.

One last test was emitted from the angry hand of Godzilla. "Rehan," she said with a sneer. I peered over, marveling at Rehan's C-.

"Damn," he muttered.

I placed a serious hand on his shoulder. "I'm proud of you, bro. I expected worse."

| MISFIT MOTIVATION |

The Misfit mindset requires fortitude There's a lot below the surface concerning how people respond to you Bro, don't take things personally Burn sage and clear your mind

---

STEM RELIEF

Mr. Faizan wore a mahogany corduroy jacket, putting us young bucks to shame. "Hisham, I'd like to further discuss your lockbox. I sense a flaw."

Instantly annoyed because this old dude was reading my mind, I froze. "I ... have some ideas, yeah."

Seriously, that was my response? After being up all night and surviving Godzilla, I couldn't unleash the floodgates?

"Well, then," Mr. Faizan said. "Speak."

My stomach flipped in frustration, and I thought of Shirley. Then my mind switched to Mohammad, and I replied, "Crap."

Mr. Faizan's face twisted quizzically. "What was that?"

"I said … *crap*. The invention is crap. With the weight sensor that seals the door, a squirrel could get inside and be trapped."

Mr. Faizan scratched his chin and looked off into the distance, pondering this response. "And what can we do about it?"

I willed the floodgates to break, even if they released a faint river. "Sir, I don't have the perfect answer yet. There are several ideas in my head that I had nightmares about at midnight. None of these are yet meeting my quality standards, but if you've taught me anything, it's that I must keep asking questions over and over again."

Alexis looked at me like Ariel from *The Little Mermaid*, stunned and wanting to be part of my world.

I waited in anticipation for Mr. Faizan's response. "Fantastic. And how will you come to a conclusion, Hisham?"

This was the predominant conundrum. After several gulps, I replied, "I have no friggin' clue."

| MISFIT MOTIVATION |

Having no friggin' clue is legit, and admitting to that is only a strength Through the process of innovation, admitting that you don't know is ironically a superhero cape that must be worn with pride

---

FAKE AWAKE

As I failed to keep my eyes open due to exhaustion, Mr. Faizan bypassed my insecurity and held up Alexis's patent certificate. STEM class stared at it like the golden ticket at Willy Wonka's chocolate factory. The Faizan monologue began as such:

"Patents are given for new and useful inventions. You'll notice Alexis's name here," he said, pointing beneath the US seal of approval.

"Then the patent number and grant date. It takes quite a while to receive a patent, and almost 99.9 percent of the time, it is turned down at first."

Mikhail raised his hand. "Why?"

"Because it must be unique by their standards. Often, there are too many other inventions that are the same."

I fought against my boredom by thinking of my lockbox. How many other loner kids had stayed up all night terrified that a squirrel would get caught? According to Mr. Faizan, many people could potentially have had this same horrifying thought, and for a fleeting moment, I felt a connection to humanity.

This brief, uplifting feeling ended when Mr. Faizan said, "If you wish to seek a patent like Alexis—"

She giggled with pride and interjected, "The invention keeps avocados fresh for thirty days!"

"—then we begin with problem *generation* to find solutions no one looks for."

Mikhail dropped his forehead to the table in communal exhaustion. I had to raise my hand, hoping my question would resuscitate the poor kid. "Man, why you gotta *generate* problems?"

Mr. Faizan gave that *I-know-your-father-and-I-know-where-you-live* look. "Pardon me, Hisham. I meant problem *identification*." (He must have had a Freudian slip.) "Then, we find the very best solution and seek a patent before focusing on commercialization ... the patent is only the beginning," Brown Einstein declared.

Mikhail, face still flat on his desk, said the unthinkable: "I'd like to design a nuclear bomb."

I knew it came from Mikhail's mental shutdown, but Mr. Faizan remained upbeat in the wake of the terrifying words uttered by my peer. "Mikhail, you could not secure a patent for that. When it comes to commercialization, if the idea is too dangerous or there's not the proper equipment, it won't be patented. Similarly, you cannot patent a vaccine or something like that. As we seek problems here in STEM, we must also filter out problems that can't be commercialized."

"I just want to be rich," Mikhail muttered in his catatonic state. I think I saw some drool.

Mr. Faizan bad-assed the moment as only he could. "Mikhail, solving small problems can make you rich, if you understand the process."

––––––––––––––– | MISFIT MOTIVATION | –––––––––––––––

Spoiler alert: it's not about money, but the money is nice Entrepreneurship and innovation are about creation, and this gives an immense sense of purpose But let's also allow Mikhail to be our spirit animal and admit that we'd all like to be rich

SOLVING REAL GIRL PROBLEMS

Terrible sleep again. Squirrel nightmares. Tomorrow couldn't have come sooner, and it arrived like the earth rotates around the sun.

I prepared for sudden death in math class as ﷺ (Angel) Maryam turned to some random dude on her right and said, "I ordered new markers online, but they never showed up …"

I watched with keen interest as she spoke to the horrible, nameless guy who didn't deserve to hear her voice. "That sucks," he replied, trying to sound cool.

"Yeah." She fluttered her lashes and took out an old marker, doodling on the page. "I bought them on Amazon. They were supposed to be fancy. Pastel colors, you know. Amazon said they arrived, but I never found the box."

As her old marker created no color on the page, my life was forever changed. Mr. Faizan had been right all along. Solving small problems and making patents from them was the answer to winning Maryam's heart. This was an epiphany. A game changer. I turned to Rehan, whose eyes were wide like he'd felt the tsunami of truth as well.

"Bro, say something to her," he implored.

"Nuh, bro."

"Bro?"

"Bro!"

I chose to remain silent. I chose to sit with the answer to Maryam's problem in a state of quiet dignity. One day, she'd see that I solved her problem, but for now, my inner James Bond sat ... patiently. I sketched the design for a marker-refill apparatus and desperately worked on my lockbox schematics.

As Maryam turned, her hijab gently cascading along her perfect face, she asked, "Did you say something, Hisham?"

Shit. No! Floodgates: "I've actually read that eleven to twelve billion articles are stolen from porches each year. Seventy percent of the population has experienced porch piracy."

She appeared annoyed. I didn't blame her. "Really, even just stealing markers?"

"They were high-quality markers."

"How do you know that?"

"Because you deserve no less."

I didn't see Rehan's eyes roll into the back of his head; I *heard* them do so. I sat petrified, knowing that my inner Outsider had stormed the castle of invisibility again when Maryam turned away.

| MISFIT MOTIVATION |

Solving small problems is a big deal. Don't begin your innovative process by focusing on satellites (although you certainly can! Start with small problems and know that innovation of these problems makes a huge impact. And it impresses the girl who spent money on pastel markers because the basic markers she had ran out of ink, and there was a way to prevent all this nonsense (Sorry Floodgates)

OVER THE EDGE

Shirley ate her Healthy Choice chicken soup as I contemplated why she tortured herself like that. More importantly, I had an announcement to make. I placed the sketch of my lockbox on the CPA break room table and turned to Mohammad.

"Is It crap?" I asked, mustering my fortitude, knowing this was the definitive moment.

Mohammad inspected the drawing with a mesmerized look on his face. "Not crap," he replied, shaking his head.

It was the nicest thing anyone had ever said to me. "Not crap" was now my mantra in life. If I could be a superhero, my name would be Not Crap. Perhaps it could be the name of a company one day. Not Crap, Inc. The world opened up, and I was on my way to becoming a man.

"I think this is very good idea," Omar chimed in.

Ralph replied as only Ralph could. "Hisham, you're a brilliant young man. This invention is incredibly useful, and I would purchase the product. There's a reason your father wanted you to come here. Learning about finance is something you need in your back pocket. You're an inventor and an innovator. Not a CPA. But having this background knowledge will help you to navigate countless situations."

We nodded at one another with the most profound, speechless Outsider understanding. I imagined that Ralph couldn't speak much in his normal life either, but once he was inspired, he waxed poetic like Shakespeare. I could relate.

Shirley asked, "What will you do next, Hisham? How does the process go from here?"

I unleashed the golden truth for the second time in two days: "I have no friggin' clue."

--------------------------| MISFIT MOTIVATION |--------------------------

*As you already know, it's great to have no friggin' clue. That means that there's a door to be opened, and if you can't open it, unleash your Misfit chainsaw and find what's on the other side (A chainsaw is pretty graphic, but find a **method** to open the door!)*

SEEKING A CLUE

Storming into Mr. Faizan's office, I dropped my sketch on his desk like a baller and proclaimed, "I want to patent this."

"You've finally come to your senses."

"I've discovered that the motion sensor that closes the lid could be accompanied by a weight sensor inside for when an animal is trapped. If there's movement in the box, the lid will open again."

"What if you order Mexican jumping beans on Amazon?"

Well played. NASA's wizarding Gandalf could come up with a million problems. I called his bluff. "There could be a heat sensor as well, sensing a live creature."

He nodded his head. "Very good, Hisham."

The scene was beginning to look very *Star Wars*, but I remained resolute and calm in front of Obi-Wan Kenobi.

Still, the matter was serious. "How do we make this happen?"

"We'll need to select a patent agent, someone who has knowledge in patent law. They'll also need to understand the technicalities behind your invention. This lawyer will help us draft the application."

There could not possibly have been a more unglamorous response. I wanted to go underground. Black market. Hand some dude my napkin idea and then be delivered a certificate followed by him saying, "You are now a millionaire." Sadly, this was not the case.

"Where do I find such an attorney?"

Mr. Faizan rifled through his desk and pushed a business card toward me, fulfilling all my this-is-sketchy black market dreams. "I have some homework for you."

Looking at the old-person business card, I resigned myself. "Cool, so like, call him tomorrow?"

"Yes, but, Hisham …" Mr. Faizan leaned forward with intent, his face expressing that he was about to share the news that a beloved pet had died. "It will cost upward of eighteen thousand dollars."

—————————— | MISFIT MOTIVATION | ——————————

Solving real-world problems takes time and dedication,
but when it comes to turning these ideas into reality,
you'll be charged for it. I hate to get all Dad here,
but you need to spend money to make money.

DESPERATELY MISSING INNOCENCE

Where I found myself next was embarrassing AF. Mr. Faizan and I sat on the park swings eating ice cream. As I rocked back and forth in shame, I needed to clarify the feelings behind this childish outdoor excursion. "Eighteen thousand dollars? Alexis's dad must be rich or something."

Mr. Faizan swung peacefully, as though he lived in *The Sound of Music*. "This is the reality, Hisham. There are so many steps to achieving what you want. Business, finance, and even innovation all come at a price."

The burning question overwhelmed me. "Why do I have to pay to be paid?"

Mr. Faizan took a bite of mint chocolate chip as he pondered. "Hisham, it's the very nature of our world. What you pay for is always an investment ... when you make the right choices. If you pay for your education, that's an investment in the future. If you pay for high-quality food, that's also an investment. You *pay* for a patent. You pay to receive what you want."

"Tickets to a Taylor Swift concert?" This was so embarrassing that I just kept swinging in shame.

Mr. Faizan's response was more serious than I'd hoped. "Hisham, that is not an investment. It has the potential to make you dance like there's no tomorrow."

I stared at him for several moments. Mr. Faizan had way too much wisdom about this topic.

"The conversation has gone in the wrong direction," I replied with dignity.

"Hisham, I will pay for it."

I thought, *My Taylor Swift ticket? Wait, no! Stop thinking this way!* "For what?"

"The patent."

يا إلهي. (Oh my God.). The cone dropped from my hand into the dirt. "What's that?" I asked.

"I will pay for it. This is your first patent."

I oscillated above the sand in juvenile shock. No one had ever done anything like this for me before, except my dad, who'd paid for my whole existence.

"Do you think the patent will get approved?"

"I've told you the statistics, but I have a feeling this is different."

Off in the distance, a squirrel ate something random with complete and utter freedom. A sign …

"Dude, I'm not gonna lie, I'm scared to even talk to a lawyer."

"Hisham, that's because you need to learn to speak."

————————— | MISFIT MOTIVATION | —————————

You need a lawyer. We all wish entrepreneurship was just some fun underground shit, but it's not true You'll also need an investor. Lastly, you need someone annoying like Mr. Faizan—someone so skilled at being annoying because they're telling you the truth

So much of innovation is about actively seeking out the problems and asking *why*. You might need to create a hundred solutions for any one problem. Being an entrepreneur isn't just about becoming a millionaire; it's about harnessing a voracious mindset for fixing something and finding multiple alternatives. (It's never ending.) Imagination at work is the first step. Learning the practicalities comes next.

The sticker shock when applying for a patent was a reality check. We have to pay to become Misfit Moguls, and we can't do it alone. There's a very good chance you have absolutely no money, but there's nothing wrong with that or living off ramen. Once you have your innovation, seek every solution you can find to jump the hurdles and take yourself to the next step.

It's hard when you're a kid, but everything you do right now with your imagination and thoughts is an investment in your future. Literally everything. I'm still a kid, but I gravitate toward adults. I'm interested in what they share. There's a practical reason for this: they teach me real-world advice that Godzilla can't.

Mohammad is the barometer for what is crap and what isn't. Omar just busts Mohammad's balls, but it's nice to be present for that. Mr. Faizan likes to go on the swings, which makes no sense, but the most important takeaway from all of this is: I was being pushed to speak.

Invisible Homework

Have a snack. I would recommend Takis, but that's not for everyone. Then sketch some stuff on the next page or write a love letter to your Maryam.

Notes 'n' Stuff:

SPEAKING WITH ... DISTINCTION?

Your ingenuity speaks louder than words...
but you still have to use words

The break room of a law firm was a far different experience from the CPA offices. There was no Mohammad, Omar, Ralph, or my beloved Shirley. There was just one white dude named Rex. Although Soraya (and every other person at school, for that matter) was terrifying, T-Rex put them all to shame.

"What's your *intention* behind this *invention*, young man?"

The play on words was very good, but I was unable to compliment Rex because I was petrified. "People don't ..." This was gonna be bad. I knew it. "People don't steal shit no more with this ... thing."

There was 100 percent no visible response or movement on his face. "I see. We'll need to do some investigation to make sure there's no other similar product. We'll also need to hash out the manufacturing process. Very rarely does a patent get approved on the first try. USPTO will scrutinize every variable. It must be entirely unique to receive a certificate."

"And from there?"

Rex gazed at me with pity. "It is only the beginning. There are many next steps."

It was as though Mr. Faizan had transported his thoughts into Mr. T-Rex. What were all these magical, mysterious steps that I didn't want to execute? I used my best adult voice to respond, "I see."

"Hisham, your father is a colleague of mine, as is Mr. Faizan."

Why did everyone know my father and Mr. Faizan? This could turn into a Mafia-like situation.

"I see."

"I believe that we can bring this patent to fruition, but they both asked that I guide you through the whole process."

"I see. So, you submit it online?"

Rex, even more placid and cold (if that was even possible), flatly replied, "Indeed. For eighteen thousand dollars."

A devilish grin came to my lips at the memory of Mr. Faizan with his ice cream cone. "I've got the cash, bro."

—————— | MISFIT MOTIVATION | ——————

"I've got the cash" is a pleasing statement

STEM MELTDOWN

As I sat in STEM the following day, analyzing an electric car and every variable that would make it problematic combined with every variable that could work, Mr. Faizan halted the class.

"Let's do a check-in," he said, pulling the righteous cap from his marker and writing on the whiteboard:

Existing solutions are the number one killer of a new solution.

He turned back to the class. "This is why innovation takes so much time. Identify a problem and try to find a solution, but more commonly than not ..."

Mr. Faizan wrote once again on the board.

The solution is already available.

"What happens next is that the idea is dropped and the inventor gives up, yes? Someone else has invented it. If a problem exists and the solution also exists, what does that tell us about the solution? It simply tells us the solution isn't good enough. As you might have discovered with today's exercise, it's very hard to innovate the electric car. Tesla has done it for you."

I shook my head in dismay and raised my hand. All eyes on me, I tried to muster the floodgates. "I … see possible improvements."

In truth, I knew that there needed to be a better battery to ensure that EV cars remained in demand to save our planet. The EV manufacturers would need to keep up their production to meet this demand while finding innovation all the time. Production needed to happen faster, and the cars needed to be lighter.

"What improvements did you find, Hisham?"

I looked down at my notes, which also contained scribbles of trees and even a samurai sword. Perhaps I'd need therapy for that. There were in fact twenty ideas that I had, but as my hand shook and blood came from my nose, falling onto the notes, I did the best I could to respond.

"It can just be better, bro."

Mr. Faizan sighed and turned back to the whiteboard with the composed frustration of a NASA dude about to lose his mind.

———————— | MISFIT MOTIVATION | ————————

There are amazing ideas inside you. Sometimes they can be verbalized, and sometimes they can't. All the same, don't let go of the ideas.

A METHODOLOGY FOR TEENAGE WORRYING

"Anytime you investigate preexisting solutions, and you see flaws, it's an innovation opportunity." He wrote those two fateful words on the whiteboard that only Allah could have created: *The Methodology*.

Mikhail sat in awe, Alexis appeared on the verge of tears, but I was bored.

"We analyze all existing solutions and find the pros and cons. What works with the existing solution, and where are the gaps? What is not working in the existing solution?"

I am not even lying; some mesmerized kid pulled out a bag of popcorn from his backpack. I had no idea who that kid was, and he completely ignored me all the time, but he was my spirit animal at that moment.

Mr. Faizan went to his computer and projected his screenshot onto the whiteboard. (I instantly thought of a hundred solutions to this Old School projection problem.)

He pointed to the screen. "As you know, the *methodology* is the only path to innovation."

"*Really?*" I muttered, having heard it a hundred times.

"Don't be a Misfit, Hisham," Mr. Faizan replied.

I could have been offended, but the guy did pay for my patent process, so I let this go. Soraya would never conceivably buy me a bag of popcorn.

The monologue continued (if you have popcorn, please reach for it). "There are two ways for people to think. There's something called a layman's response to the problem by someone who is *not* an innovator, and so they start thinking in one direction to solve the problem. Then they immediately jump to the other direction of the problem. Lastly, they jump to the next direction of the problem. They keep on thinking *around* the problem without going anywhere, but there's a word in English for this type of thinking: *worrying*."

It was legit. I worried more than anyone.

As this rhetoric continued in the background, I began to analyze the problem of Maryam ignoring me from every different angle.

"Maryam Ignoring Me" Root Cause Problems:

1. *I'm too skinny*

2. *I don't have enough money*

3. *I'm not funny*

4. *She likes that weird guy who sits next to her in math class*

5. *Our parents haven't arranged our marriage*

6. *Lesbian, maybe? (Totally okay, if so)*

7. *She's focused on school*

8. *She's not properly fed*

9. *She's blind and cannot see me*

10. *She doesn't know I like her*

11. *Rehan speaks to her in private and tells her how much I'm into her, and therefore she's not attracted to what she can have*

Mr. Faizan continued to rattle on like an adult in a Charlie Brown cartoon, and I went in with my solutions.

"Maryam Ignoring Me" Starbursting Introspection—Yellow Flavor Solutions:

1. *Take creatine, lift, and get huge*

2. *Finish my patent, create a business, buy a Lambo*

3. *Learn some jokes*

4. *Take down that math class guy*

5. *Bribe the matchmaker.*

6. *I simply had no appropriate response to #6 in my previous list. More power to her.*

7. *Help her with her homework. Or just do it altogether.*

8. *Feed her fresh Pakistani food.*

9. *Create an invention to help.*

10. *This one was the hardest of all. I had no idea how to speak with her.*

11. *Most importantly, give Rehan the stink eye.*

The top secret methodology asked me to investigate each of these solutions, but before I could get to work, Mr. Faizan said, "Class, I see that you're all in need of fresh air."

I'm sure it was me he was speaking to directly because my brain was spent.

─────── | MISFIT MOTIVATION | ───────

Any methodology will drive you insane, but this one can be applied to real-world and real-life problems. Learn the steps, but the biggest takeaway is that it can help you solve any problem. You don't need to analyze a satellite. You can problem solve elements of your Invisible existence.

THE GARDEN OF TRANQUILITY AND TURMOIL

Mr. Faizan led weary students to the STEM garden where I witnessed a happy bluebird chirping. My anxiety was immediately quelled until the bird soared into the sky and shat on my arm. I tried to play this off as I brought a napkin to my bloody nose.

As we all stood awkwardly, not knowing what to do, Mr. Faizan calmly placed his hands in his pockets and looked up toward the sky. His timing was better than mine because the bluebird had flown away.

"Sometimes we need to clear our minds. The mind isn't working at an optimal performance level if we're sitting in a classroom all day. Moments like this, in nature ..." (It was as though he thought we were in the rainforest or something.) "These moments remind us to slow down and allow our ideas to sink in, as well as our problem-solving skills."

"Legit," Mikhail responded.

"Hisham, as we rest, would you like to tell the class about your recent meeting with a patent attorney?"

Shit. "Yeah, I, um ... I told him ... I told him I got the cash."

The class snickered, but it was the truth. My ability to speak to T-Rex had been so abominable that those were the most profound words I'd shared with him, even though we still managed the patent process together.

Mr. Faizan whispered, "Speak. You must learn to speak."

"I, uh, showed him the design, and to quote Mikhail, he thought it was legit. So we ... locked it down."

Mr. Faizan nodded in approval, encouraging me to say more. "And what does that process look like, Hisham?"

With bird shit on my arm and a bloody napkin in my hand, I closed my eyes and willed the floodgate gods to be with me now. When I opened my eyes, I unleashed.

"Sir, there's a utility patent and a design patent. One is for a new invention, and the other is for the look of it. I have applied for both for my lockbox, as design and function were both deemed unique after a search for similar inventions. Furthermore, this is not a provisional patent, which you'd apply for if you're still working on the design and want to protect your idea. In this case, the design is done."

Mr. Faizan pushed me further. "And how long is a provisional patent good for?"

This dude was calling my bluff, and I had him. "This lasts for a year. You're basically protecting yourself from competitors."

"Do you see, Hisham? You can speak when you will yourself to do so." Obi-Wan had me again. "And how did you learn about this process?"

Through this one-upmanship, I knew that he wanted me to say it was T-Rex. "I memorized it from LegalZoom, sir."

Victory was mine.

─────── | MISFIT MOTIVATION | ───────

To file for a patent, you need a title, your personal information, a summary of the invention and what it does, a description, a drawing, and a shitload of money. When in doubt, check out LegalZoom, but you stand a better chance if you hire a heavy hitter.

REALITY CHECK

That evening as night descended, I stepped into Dad's office and contemplated whether I was already prepared to file my second patent for the streetlamp that would increasingly get brighter and keep me up at night.

"Dad?"

"Yes, Hisham."

"Have you heard anything … about my patent application?" It was a valid inquiry. I'd gone through the process (it didn't take long) and forked over the cash to T-Rex. Surely, my dad must have heard by now.

There was the ominous swivel of his chair and the customary spreadsheet on his desktop. In moments such as these, I considered it to be something of an Ahmad family campfire.

"Son, these things take time."

Time? This was preposterous! "A few days? Weeks?" Was someone keeping me out of the loop?

My father sighed. "It could be years."

My Misfit mind said *fuuuuuck*, and the sorta rad patina of being an Outsider went dim. I felt more Invisible than ever—a pawn, a cog in the wheel, a nobody—all because I didn't possess an ounce of patience.

"Can we, um, expedite the process?"

"We cannot. It's out of our hands now. Mr. Faizan, T-Rex, and I have deemed the invention to be quite unique, and we agree that it has a fantastic chance of being approved."

Okay, I only had to pause for a sec because my dad referred to the lawyer as T-Rex without mentioning my inner thoughts. It was strange, and I concluded that my dad and I were biologically entwined and somehow shared the same brain.

"I see. I'll be patient," I promised.

——————— | MISFIT MOTIVATION | ———————

Being approved for a patent can take a long time, perhaps years. Only the chosen ones get approved quickly. That's a bit of foreshadowing...

THE MELTDOWN

Two minutes later, I was on the kitchen landline with Mr. Faizan, seated on the floor with my back against the cabinets. "Bro, years? Like literally, wait for years?"

"Calm down, Hisham."

"I won't calm down—this is lame!"

If I thought the swing set interlude had been embarrassing, this was completely mortifying. Not only was I on a landline (my father still wouldn't allow me to have a phone), but I was also curling my finger around the twisty cord in sheer anger.

"Hisham, listen to me. You're learning all of these aspects at once, and you sound stressed. Your napkin ideas will get patented, one at a time, but you must learn about the finance and the law, and go through the process. You must also understand that there's a system in place, and systems take very much time."

I channeled the wisdom of Mohammad. "Crap. It's just crap."

When I said *crap*, I meant crap. This needed to go faster. How long did Alexis's patent take? Did she apply when she was four? This needed to happen before I graduated from high school so that Maryam could see. I *needed* to start a business and show up for senior year in my Lamborghini. Maybe a Ferrari. Maybe both on separate days.

In hindsight, I truly believed in my idea, and my excitement for the outcome was wrecking my teenage soul.

"Slow down," Mr. Faizan cautioned. "You're already ahead of the game. You're learning each of these processes. You're gaining knowledge that most other students don't have."

In my best *wah wah wah* voice, I replied, "Because the system is designed to make me a good employee, I know."

There was silence on the other end, and I feared that my sarcasm had gone too far. "Hisham, I want you to do me a favor."

Buy you tickets to Taylor Swift?

"What is that?"

"The University of Texas, Dallas (UTD), has asked for a STEM student to speak to their business class. I'm quite close with the dean of the program, and he'd like his students to understand the benefit of practical knowledge."

"No."

"Yes."

"No."

"Write a brief speech. This is important, Hisham. It's a great step in your learning."

All kinds of conspiracy theories swam through my head. I was being groomed to be the brown Steve Jobs or Elon Musk; Faizan and my dad would take the cash and move to Dubai and hit the casinos. I'd be slaving away, making inventions for the crown prince of Saudi Arabia while beauties in burkas sat on their laps.

Still, I acquiesced. "Fine. But you suck," was my adult reply.

─────── | MISFIT MOTIVATION | ───────

Being impatient is okay and understandable
In fact, it's very much a part of the Misfit spirit

PATENT ANXIETY

Within moments, Rehan arrived at my door with an open bag of Cool Ranch Doritos. As he licked his fingers, I squirmed in disgust; I hated when people did that.

"Can I come in, bro?"

I was spent. "No, you cannot."

"That's rude, man."

"Go home."

His eyes lit up. "I had Maryam's fact tattooed on my left pec!"

As the villain slowly lowered the collar of his shirt to reveal this work of art, I slammed the door right in his face, feeling on the verge of tears. There was a gentle knock after that act of bro violence. "I was kidding, Hisham! I was just kidding!" Rehan pleaded.

Slowly opening the door again, I peered through the crack with one saddened eye. "That was messed up," I said.

"I wanted your attention. I missed you ..." Rehan extended the bag of Doritos in solidarity.

"So sketchy, bro. I saw you yesterday."

Rehan tried to piss me off with the most romantic sarcasm I'd ever heard come from anyone other than myself. "Tomorrow was forever ago."

I rolled my eyes and acquiesced. It was well played, so I gave him props.

As we walked up to my room and then situated ourselves, the dread of writing my speech brought me back to the holy grail. I read aloud from *Rich Dad Poor Dad* to Rehan as he sat on my oversized beanbag, playing Nintendo.

"So, what kind of assets am I suggesting that you or your children acquire?

+ Businesses that do not require my presence
+ Stocks
+ Bonds
+ Income-generating real estate
+ Notes (IOUs)
+ Royalties from intellectual property such as music, scripts, and patents
+ Anything else that has value, produces income or appreciates, and has a ready market"[6]

Rehan didn't even glance at me. "Dude, you're crazy or something."

"Mr. Kiyosaki is a legend, bro. You just don't get it." I reached for the bag of Doritos (no doubt covered in Rehan's germs) and played it off casually, as I always did, but deep down, I was distracting myself from public speaking anxiety and trying to please my dad one story below.

---

6   Kiyosaki, *Rich Dad Poor Dad.*

"You need a girlfriend."

"I can't have one. I need a wife."

"Well then, get the matchmaker working overtime because you're losing your mind."

I was torn at this point. My patent anxiety was pissing me off. I'd put myself out there, but all I was hearing were tumbleweeds. Okay, I wanted to learn—wanted to please them so badly—but I also hoped to be a kid who didn't feel the sudden onslaught of a migraine from worrying about a nosebleed.

I returned my attention to *Rich Dad Poor Dad*. "Royalties from intellectual property such as music, scripts, and patents." The final word hit me like a train. The word *patent* was now like the name of a girl who dumped me because she said I had bad teeth or something.

I had to come clean. "It's crazy waiting on this patent."

Rehan clicked away at the wireless controller. "I know what you should patent."

"More designs?"

"No, bro. You should patent your virginity because that shit is timeless."

I sidestepped this insult by staring at the handheld video game controller, pondering how the buttons could be rearranged so that Rehan would one day actually win a game. Then I returned my attention to my speech for the University of Texas, Dallas.

———————————— | MISFIT MOTIVATION | ————————————

As Mr. Kiyosaki says, "The rich focus on their asset columns while everyone else focuses on their income statements." More importantly, it's a fact that Rehan will never win at Nintendo. My innovations can't help him.

———————————————————————————————————————

7   Kiyosaki, *Rich Dad Poor Dad.*

PHOENIX BACK IN THE FLAMES

A week later, standing backstage at the university auditorium, I gave Mr. Faizan a side glare that could have burned a bridge. There was a clamor from the audience, as my entrance was delayed for five minutes due to dry mouth and flop sweat.

"You can do this, Hisham. Share your speech."

I whispered to him, "I have nothing to share with these …"—I went for humor—"peasants."

Mr. Faizan didn't appreciate this statement.

"Hisham, come on now."

My legs shook and my heart pounded as I listened to the large auditorium of students chatting and waiting for me. I held my speech in my sweaty hand while I reasoned that I was in a state that Rehan would call "shitting the bed."

"I can't do this, Mr. Faizan," I pleaded, grabbing his hands like someone about to bungee jump.

"You can."

"No, no. I'm sick. I have … bronchitis." It was a last-ditch effort.

"I believe in you, Hisham."

From the look in his eye, I knew he was serious. There are moments in everyone's lives when the terror is so great that you're pretty sure you're about to die, but for whatever reason, I released Mr. Faizan's hands and felt one foot step onto the stage, and then the other, and then on repeat.

As I approached the microphone, I instantly caught the image of Rehan at the back of the auditorium. He was cracking up (son of a …). After his laughter subsided, he warmly smiled and lifted a big thumbs-up into the air. And so I was ready to begin.

"Good afternoon, my name is Hisham Ahmad."

There was faint applause, and perhaps a tumbleweed rolled by. Then there were crickets. I looked to Rehan once more for assurance, and he rolled his hand forward in a circle, like someone backstage at a television news program willing me to fill airtime.

"I guess … I guess it's kinda weird that I'm here. I'm just a kid, and you are business students."

Mr. Faizan called from the side stage, "You are a STEM legend!"

More faint applause. I shook my head. This shit show needed to end.

"Are there any questions?"

Audience members looked from side to side. They expected me to speak, and I simply couldn't. I reasoned that there was no hope. My patent would die, I'd puke on stage, and Maryam would have an arranged marriage with that math class dude.

Still, I stood there, ready for what was to come.

———————————| MISFIT MOTIVATION |———————————

When you freeze up, request that people ask questions.

CUE SUPERHERO STRENGTH

A girl raised her hand and jumped up and down. "Hisham, what brought you to STEM?" she slurred and gazed upon me like a true Belieber. With my laser vision, I saw her drop a bottle of Mike's Hard Lemonade. As it rolled below the seats, I did not judge this beautiful girl. Her cleavage was immense, and my teenage face flushed.

"My dad." I nervously grinned into the mic. A few others laughed with me, but my eyes were still on her chest, so I barely noticed.

"And what have you *learned*? I never went to STEM, but I'm interested in *business* … obviously." I knew what *business* she spoke of and hoped Mr. Faizan would not dive in before me.

The hot, drunk girl brought out my inner Thor. I pulled out my flashcard and proceeded to speak like a half-dead robot.

"They say … um … they say embracing the power of knowledge is the key to unlocking your greatest potential. I call nonsense." I heard the crickets again and tried something different.

I went in for the kill.

"Bullshit!"

The audience gasped, and I went on. "That's what someone with zero practical experience would say. Real-life skills that you *actually* benefit from are not taught at school because the schooling system is producing … employees. You do as you're told, you don't take any chances, and your math teacher ruins your life."

The continued laughter spurred me on once more.

"It's not a bad thing to follow instructions … um … but in doing what you're *told* all the time, your creativity is *impeded*." I had written that word into the speech to be fancy and make Rehan roll his eyes. "You're not questioning, and I don't blame you because the system is designed to disable … um … curiosity."

Rehan rolled his eyes! I could see it from afar. He emitted the sweet sound of friendship: "Bro!" It reverberated through the halls.

"Shit, sorry. Mr. Faizan wanted me to say all that." I turned to the side, and now it was Mr. Faizan rolling his eyes. I crumpled the notecard and dug deep. "Seriously, though, I had a rough time in school. I still do. I've, um …" As I grasped the microphone, the floodgates were unleashed as though Allah once again coursed through me. "I was picked on a lot. Being a brown kid in Texas isn't easy. I think I channeled all of this into, like, books and stuff? I memorized so much shit."

The next silence from the audience was different. They were with me. I sank into a weird sense of confidence that felt like a rare

Outsider disease. "That stuff is important, but we never use it. Innovation is what runs our world. It always has, so why is the system not built for us to innovate? I mean, businesses and finance run our world, but we're not given the chance with this knowledge at an early age, I guess. Mr. Faizan taught me that we're trained to be employees, and we *need* our employees."

As I looked out into a crowd of stunned faces, I didn't know if it was tears or a nosebleed coming, but I pushed through. "But you're not here because you want to be a good employee. You're here to change the world—a world that we're all trying to … um … um, make better?"

I felt the mythical bluebird on my shoulder, full of real-life shit to share. "Many of you might feel like Outsiders. You're screwing up and pissing off your parents, but you're here." I placed my finger on the podium with uncharacteristic power that felt corny as hell. "You're *here* because you want to do better for yourselves and others. And the temporary pains, maybe feeling Invisible or unworthy, are the emotions that spark innovation in the world— innovation in *yourself*."

I stepped back from the podium feeling utterly exposed. After a pause, the audience rose to their feet and applauded. It was the moment that would forever change my life. Except that the hot girl in the audience was gone … and I dreamt of reaching that profound age of eighteen to stand a chance.

As Mr. Faizan came out and put the expected manly hand communicating *you did good, but it would be awkward to hug you* on my shoulder, he said, "You did an amazing job, Hisham."

Through my exhilaration, I replied, "Made that shit up, bro. I just pretended I was you."

He warmly smiled. "That fills me with pride."

Through my triumph, the faux Kardashian captivated my thoughts. "Cool and all, but I gotta go find that drunk girl with the hourglass figure."

Calmly walking off the stage, I heard Mr. Faizan cry out, "Halt!" Impressed by the use of the word *halt*, I replied, "Yes, sir."

———————— | MISFIT MOTIVATION | ————————

You have to plug away at stepping out of your comfort zone. People can encourage you to do it, but you have to force yourself sometimes. If public speaking is hard for you, don't be afraid to feel the fear and do it anyway. Remember that when it comes to something that scares you, there are so many others who feel the same way.

People tend to worry about problems and get nowhere. That's not how an innovator thinks. True innovators use an excruciating ... methodology. They take one aspect of the problem, do the first level of analysis and then subsequent levels of analysis, draw a conclusion, and come back. This is called structured thinking. But how the hell are we supposed to do that when we're thinking of a hundred other things and aren't even adults yet? We *force* ourselves, just as we must force ourselves to do all the other smart things we don't want to do.

We also must force ourselves to speak. Even if the older girl in the audience with the tremendous figure lends you conviction, you'll have to push through a number of barriers and feel the discomfort of speaking and having her disappear. This can be said for almost every state of innovation. You're not going to be comfortable all the time. You'll doubt yourself and hate everyone for doing the same, but this time spent stepping out of your comfort zone is an *investment* in your Outsider future. Having people believe in you is huge, but sometimes you must do things for yourself.

If I was using the *methodology* to dig deeper into my Maryam solutions, I'd present more problems for each solution:

1. I could take creatine, eat a ton of beef, and still not get huge

2. I could get a Lambo, and she won't care

3. My jokes would fall flat

4. I could try to beat up the math class dude and land in the ER

5. The matchmaker might not think Maryam
   is right for me

6. Maryam could be a lesbian, and I would
   fully support her. No problem.

7. I could do all her homework, and it wouldn't
   make a difference

8. Maryam could be on a diet and refuse to
   eat my exquisite Pakistani cuisine

9. If Maryam were indeed blind, I would help her.
   No problem again.

10. If I spoke to her with the distinction of Lawrence of
    Arabia, I'd still be in a Cyrano de Bergerac situation

11. If I gave Rehan the evil eye, it would only warm
    his heart

Invisible Homework

So, you see, we find more problems within our solutions, which is messed up. However, this structured thinking is essential for innovation. Go ahead and use that one problem you've been working on and challenge your solutions. I'm sorry; it's painful. Your reality might come crashing down, so be sure to play your favorite video game after this exercise.

Notes 'n' Stuff:

7

LIGHT AT THE END OF THE TUNNEL

There's a pristine moment when
you choose to no longer be Invisible

Following my epic speech at UTD, something had broken open within. It was a combination of factors: I'd shared my boring speech, was spurred on by the hot drunk girl, and then spoke from the heart, unscripted. The raging applause at the end (only thanks to my honesty) allowed me to wake up the next morning and walk into the kitchen like I owned the place.

"Good morning, Dad," I said casually, pouring my orange juice into a glass as though it were a smooth martini.

When his newspaper came down, I sensed his confusion.

"Good morning, son. You're looking well."

"Should it come as any surprise?" I leaned my elbow onto the counter and gazed out the kitchen window, enjoying the sunshine.

Wait, this was corny as fuck … I quickly shoved the Tupperware into my backpack and resumed my normal Outsider awkwardness. "See ya!" I said with urgency, remembering again that the day held school, STEM, and Shirley and the gang.

"Wait, Hisham."

I turned back, my heart already pounding as yesterday's triumph disappeared and reality sank in. Back to the grind …

"Yes?" I asked.

"Mr. Faizan told me about your speech. What a success it was …"

Dad brought my glow back in an instant! "Thank you, yeah. It was super … um … important to me."

He smiled. "I'm proud of you, son. Very proud."

I could have passed out from the pride that I felt, but I chose to write it off. "Yeah, it was, like, pretty cool and stuff."

"You have a great day. Keep up the good work," he said as the newspaper, like a curtain, slowly came in front of his face once more.

My heart was so thoroughly warmed. Yes, I would make today a good day.

――――――― | MISFIT MOTIVATION | ―――――――

There are several moments to be cherished. You'll be acknowledged and applauded. Don't throw these moments away. The Outsider in you will call bullshit, but you need to slow down and let the triumphs sink in.

ROOT CAUSE ANALYSIS

As I sped to school, I rode my bike as if it were a Ducati, the wind flying through my hair. Something was shifting; I could just feel it. Mr. Faizan appeared on a cloud in the distance, like one of those religious paintings where a God (choose your own) bursts through the heavens as a faint glimmer.

"Hisham," Mr. Faizan said, his voice cascading through the hillsides, "Remember today … *root cause analysis.*"

This reminder from heavenly Faizan was a serious mood killer, and I nearly crashed into an old lady walking her dog. "Watch where you're going!" she screamed.

"Sorry, ma'am!" I said as I continued to speed along. The potential accident occurred for understandable reasons. I expected the deity of Faizan to say, *You'll crush this day, Hisham. You'll get the patent, get the girl, and rule the world.*

Sadly this hadn't been the case. So … my mind went to root cause analysis. The objective was all too plain: he wanted me to remember STEM research so that I'd get rich and he'd obtain his ticket to Dubai, as I've explained before.

But root cause analysis guided my mind to a different question. Why was I Invisible at school? Some might say it was a personality trait and I simply was an introvert, but the speech at UTD had taught me something new: it was because I didn't put myself out there. Today would be different. *Today*, I'd make a change.

In my mind, I made a list of frightening but necessary tasks. Number one was buying the librarian a muffin. I'd show her … show her that I'd changed since she was the one who had forced me into the quad. I had the audacity to ride my bike through the Starbucks drive-through.

As I placed the muffin on her desk, she looked up at me with sincere confusion.

"What is this?" she asked.

I had planned to be bold, but the usual tension took hold. "I … um … wanted to feed you stuff."

Nothing could have been more awkward. Where had the orator from yesterday gone? I blamed Mr. Faizan and all the root cause analysis bullshit from the sky.

The librarian lady hadn't changed one bit. "Get yourself to class, Hisham. I won't tolerate this behavior."

I fled quickly as though pursued by a velociraptor dinosaur.

When I had nearly reached the revolving doors, librarian lady called out again. "Hisham!" I turned, still embarrassed by my gesture. It was the first time I saw warmth on her angry librarian face. "Thank you for the muffin."

My heart melted for the second time today, and I was beginning to understand root cause analysis differently.

1. *Why am I a Misfit? I have no choice*

2. *Why am I an Outsider? Because I'm cool*

3. *Why am I Invisible? I've been afraid to be seen*

----------------- | MISFIT MOTIVATION | -----------------

Sometimes you want attention but aren't getting it Other times, you receive attention when you don't want it Being **seen** *begins with being heard Root cause analysis sometimes provides those moments when you're like, "Damn, that had a simple answer. I just needed to think about it"*

CONFRONTING THE DEMONS

By "confronting your demons," I mean the soda-throwing guy. This reconnaissance mission required tactical preparation, and only Rehan could give me the bad advice that I needed. But first we needed to explore my day of Misfit root cause analysis together.

We stood in front of the cafeteria microwave as my hand held my Tupperware, quaking in fear.

"No, bro. No, don't do it," Rehan said.

"Give me your Tupperware."

He shook his head in confusion. "No."

"Come on, man. We deserve this." My statement held a far greater weight than I'd anticipated as I witnessed the look of solidarity on Rehan's face. He gulped and handed me his lunch. Holding his cold haleem and my nihari, I did something I'd never done before. After opening the door to the microwave, I put our dishes inside and pressed the two-minute button.

I want to say that fireworks went off, but Rehan and I awkwardly stood there, listening to the microwave hum. As the marvelous aroma of our lunches wafted through the cafeteria, heads turned. I spotted the soda-throwing guy wearing a football jersey, no doubt made aware of my act of indecency. Once the microwave dinged, I pulled out our dishes.

"Let's go outside," Rehan implored.

"No, bro. I want to sit inside."

"Why, man? It's crazy in here."

I looked directly at Mountain Dew man and made my choice. "I'm not afraid of this shit."

Rehan walked behind me as we strode through the cafeteria. The whole thing happened in slow motion as heads turned, my shiny black hair cascaded on a breeze, and I was perhaps wearing a phantom Rolex. Perhaps the cafeteria lady fainted, the librarian sensed the moment and careened into a shelf of books, and somewhere off in the distance, Shirley put down her Lean Cuisine and fell to her knees.

As the soda guy picked up his red cup of Mountain Dew (was this a tailgate party or something?), every nerve in my body went on overdrive. The wind ceased to blow through my hair, and my imagined Rolex disappeared.

"Yeah, bro," I said to Rehan. "Let's sit outside."

OUTSIDER ACCEPTANCE

Although my move in the cafeteria hadn't been as baller as I thought it would be, I reasoned that I'd still made progress. I'd heated my lunch and walked across the room. Progress had been made …

Stepping into math class, I saw that familiar glimmer of love and contempt in Soraya's eyes, but I ignored all of this as I breathed in the beauty of Maryam in *the* pink dress—the same dress I once marveled at through the library window. She turned to me and smiled, and I nearly died. Rehan saw this interaction and elbowed my side. There was definitely something different happening in my Outsider world.

Soraya Godzilla proclaimed, "Class, before we begin, I'd like to bring something important to your attention." It occurred to me that Soraya sensed that I had an ounce of confidence today and that required some serious discussion to dispel the matter. She sipped from her Christmas cup, and I lost faith in her yet again. "I think some of you have watched Hisham's speech on YouTube."

Don't shit the bed, don't shit the bed. YouTube? What the hell?

Rehan replied to Godzilla with assurance, "I was there, ma'am."

The demon remained placid but continued to speak. "I would like Hisham to share his experience."

The whole class turned toward me, and my foray into public speaking was again being tested. I spoke with distinction: "I didn't know that was on YouTube, bro." Also, why was Soraya staying up late at night stalking me?

"The school was informed of this achievement and also the patent you're applying for."

I threw my head back like Mikhail falling asleep in STEM. This was surreal. Couldn't an Outsider have some privacy? Still, my root cause analysis day continued in full swing.

Why were people paying attention to me?

1. *I decided to not be as Invisible*

2. *I made a great speech for cleavage girl*

3. *I had a patent that I believed in, but it still might fail*

Maryam turned to me again, completely ignoring the math dude. "I saw it too," she said. "I think it's gone viral."

That was all I needed. I rose from my chair like Abraham Lincoln standing at six feet four. The phoenix was out of the ashes.

"I confess. That was me in the video."

Soraya appeared perplexed. "Hisham, I have to apologize to you." *Here we go.* I looked hot on YouTube, and now she was apologizing. "And I'd like you to draw your patent sketch on the board, using *mathematic* information, of course."

The response rapidly collected in my head, and I felt it was the greatest revenge that I could ever achieve. "I'm sorry, ma'am. That's top secret."

———— | MISFIT MOTIVATION | ————

Outsider revenge is a funny thing. It feels so good. It is redemption, justice, and finally being seen. Do be sure to James Bond your type of revenge so that it looks really cool. Going from Misfit to Mogul means you'll eventually have way more money than them. Be kind.

STEM CAUSE ANALYSIS

There's the root, and then there's the STEM (I'm so sorry; I had to).

As I sat falling asleep with boredom, Mr. Faizan continued to project onto the whiteboard and also project onto a handful of kids that he was jealous of because we had more fun.

"As you'll see," he said, walking to the whiteboard and obscuring the projection. "Heat stroke is the most serious heat-related illness. It occurs when the body can no longer control its temperature: the body's temperature rises rapidly, the sweating mechanism fails, and the body is unable to cool down. When heat stroke occurs, the body temperature can rise to 106 degrees Fahrenheit or higher within ten to fifteen minutes."

This all made perfect sense because that's the effect Maryam had on me, and during the Texas summers, I always thought I'd pass out.

"Now," Mr. Faizan went on, "look here to the weakest link: dehydration and not choosing to drink water. Why is this the weakest link?" he asked. No one raised their hand, and therefore Mr. Faizan performed his customary gesture of ruining my life. "Hisham?"

When I heard my name, I seriously felt like I'd woken up from a dream. "Um … people have underlying conditions, or they are impoverished and have no AC. It can also be because they decided to travel to the Sahara Desert, so they paid for torture."

Although I gave some plausible ideas, I noticed most of the class reaching for their water bottles.

"These are all thoughts that help us to look deeper at the problem. That is root cause analysis." Mr. Faizan leaned on his desk in that way that annoyed me but also had me taking notes to look suave one day. "Now, Hisham, since you're a YouTube sensation …" (Was everyone seriously stalking me online?) "I'd like you to come to the board and state a problem, then begin a session of root cause analysis."

Although I wanted to turn down this second offer of the day, I got up, mostly because my legs had fallen asleep and I needed to move. Once I reached the whiteboard, I covered my eyes from the glare of the projection screen, projecting onto me its sad, lonely words that even an Outsider found disheartening.

Mr. Faizan managed to turn off the projector, and I wrote with a macabre flourish:

Problem: Dead Markers.

"What do you mean by that?" he asked.

My eyelids felt heavy, but I persisted. "Markers die pretty quickly. The root cause is the design of the marker. It can only hold so much ink. It will die faster for a creative person who uses them often, which is sadly ironic. There is no way, with the current design, to refill the marker, which I believe is on purpose. Corporations make more money when consumers have to replace their markers instead of receiving a refill. A refillable marker would be less aesthetically pleasing and not carry on with a tried-and-true brand appearance."

Alexis blinked several times, and Mikhail held his hands together in prayer. I was baffled by having such reactions from people two days in a row, but it occurred to me that before my marker speech, I didn't need to stop and wait for the floodgates to open. It happened effortlessly (perhaps because I was too tired to worry).

"Go on, Hisham," Mr. Faizan said.

All at once, my Outsider/Invisible root cause analysis introspection from that morning brought me energy. I quickly resketched a napkin idea I'd found at my bedside. I must have been sleep-drawing because I couldn't remember making the sketch, but it was still fresh in my mind.

"Take, for instance, a traditional Crayola marker. In the manufacturing process, melted plastic is formed into marker 'barrels.' They're then screen-printed with the famous logo. The logo dries quickly as the marker passes through a drying tunnel. From there, the ink reservoir is inserted into the barrel as well as the color solution."

As I stood there, feeling like a rep for Crayola, the popcorn guy raised his hand. "Does the ink instantly fill the … um … barrel thing?"

"No, popcorn guy. The process takes a minute or two."

"My name is Joseph."

"Cool, nice to meet you, Joseph."

Mr. Faizan chimed in, "Hisham, I'm incredibly impressed. Where did you conduct your research?"

This was LegalZoom honestly all over again. "On their website, sir." I think that had been done while sleepwalking as well.

"I see."

"It is a fact …" I proclaimed, pointing to the ground with ferocity, as I'd performed on the UTD podium (no less pathetic on this occasion). "These markers will last for a minimum of six hundred feet."

Alexis replied with pity, "That's such a shame."

"Seems like enough to me," Mikhail responded.

"No, Alexis, you are right. Mikhail, I respect you, bro. But girls need more footage." This seemed oddly inappropriate.

"Okay, Hisham," the STEM Omar Sharif chimed in. "What can be done about it? You've expertly found the root cause, but what's your hypothesis?"

Although I had my hypothesis, I didn't see the point in answering. STEM already felt boring and mundane, just like school in general. Was I growing out of everything? Was my impatience so great that nothing could occupy my imagination?

As this worry built inside, I had to respond. "That's top secret, sir."

A world of color … for Shirley.

"No crap. No crap," Mohammad proclaimed as I showed everyone my sketch for the marker innovation.

Omar shrugged. "I agree with Mohammad. No crap."

Although this was another huge boost, it was Shirley who I wanted to impress most. She wore the sweater that I'd sketched. Apparently, she'd crocheted it within days. "Fabulous, Hisham."

"Here's my reasoning. The back of the marker barrel, which is one of the last pieces to be installed, can come off allowing for refillable ink. From there, the consumer will refill the marker without throwing it into the trash and ruining the planet. This *green* approach will boost Crayola's sales considering that 54 percent of the country is worried about climate change."

Ralph wore a bow tie that day, which made me appreciate him even more. "Hisham, does the company not have refillable markers?"

My sleepwalking research returned. "Only the Scribble Scrubbie. For all water-based markers, it's advised that you make a desperate attempt to dip the tip in warm water for about five seconds." Once again, this statement felt wildly inappropriate.

Shirley remained my beacon of light. "Hisham, you impress me every day. I just think that you're bound to be a millionaire. I would most certainly buy these earth-conscious markers, and I think every other woman would too."

That meant Maryam would buy them …

As Ralph awkwardly took out the taxation book and read aloud, changing the subject far too quickly, my mind drifted into various places. Root cause analysis:

Why am I Invisible?

1. I don't speak my mind

2. I hold back

3. I'm afraid of how people will respond to me

Why am I an Innovator?

1. My mind is on overdrive
2. I see solutions before many else do
3. It impresses Mr. Faizan

Why am I a Misfit?

1. People don't understand me
2. I have salacious thoughts
3. I'm a teenage boy

I couldn't come up with a hypothesis for most of these issues.

--- | MISFIT MOTIVATION | ---

Root cause analysis is often surprising. You unearth things that only seem obvious once you explore them. At first, this feels taxing (sorry for the pun) on the brain, but once you get used to it, the process becomes second nature

ASLEEP OR AWAKE?

As I sat once again on the kitchen floor, speaking to Mr. Faizan and twirling my finger around the twisty cord like a toddler, I wasn't sure if I was in a dream or not.

"I want you to be a leader at STEM. I've spoken with your father. I'd like you to become a partial owner and lead motivation facilitator."

Had I a beverage, I would have done a spit take. Instead, I felt my nose begin to bleed. As I reached for a paper towel, I gave a gentleman's reply: "What the f—?"

"Hisham, listen. What you did today in class captivated the students like nothing I'd ever seen before. They deeply listened to what you had to say, and you've clearly mastered the curriculum. I want you to help me make the training even better by more fully capturing the minds and hearts of our STEM students."

Everything was coming full circle. Once I'd made an intention for the day to erase my invisibility, I was now in the spotlight. I wasn't quite sure how I felt about that …

Once again, I gave a genteel response. "That's super corny, dude."

"No, Hisham, it isn't. I know what you can do. I see it every day. We can reinvent the school with your help. We need a young voice. Your video online has been viewed thousands of times. *You* can reach young kids."

"Wait. You're like a NASA genius guy and probably a millionaire …"

"I am, yes."

"So why … why …" Tears came to the surface as the reality of it all sank in. How was my life moving ahead so fast? Why was everyone suddenly impressed by me? How was my invisibility melting away? (And where was my fucking patent?)

With all these questions in mind, I simply asked, "Why me?"

"Because I wholeheartedly believe in you."

| MISFIT MOTIVATION |

Guys, I cannot overstate how important it is to find the people who believe in you. They will change your life. To get all Mafia about this again: find "your people." La tua gente شعبك. 你的人. Votre peuple

---

You catch my drift.

Once you identify problems and make a laundry list of solutions, root cause analysis takes you a bit further. It helps you to explore *why* something is happening. I didn't go from Invisible to innovator overnight, but examining the root cause of why I felt Invisible led to rapid change. Also, examining the root cause of why I wasn't a millionaire inventor came down to the same brainstorming, and not to beat a dead horse (that's a terrible phrase, BTW), but many of the answers arise from learning about the stuff that we're not taught in school—innovation, the patent process, finance aspects, and as you'll soon see, business know-how.

We, the Invisible ones (sounds like a treatise or something), rule the world. Not because we're seeking power or fame, but because our crazy loner ideas mean something and have true potential. These get shot down throughout life as dragon/Godzilla Sorayas and Mountain Dew guys mess us up. I cannot explain enough how important it is to stay Invisible if that's protecting you, but when the time is right, allow yourself to be seen. Bro, all the chicks go for the geeks later in life. We're the ones who held to our ideas and made them happen. I haven't experienced this phenomenon yet, but I've done the research.

Invisible Homework

- Sometimes, the answer to *how* is *why*. It sounds profound because it is. Root cause analysis (boring AF) holds a lot of weight. We can sit around worrying about problems without searching for the reasons behind the problems.

- For this exercise, you can choose the innovation kicking around in your head or a life problem you're working on. List all the reasons *why*. What's the background? Note: this work is quite soothing, so if you're that type of person, you might brew some tea and light a candle.

Notes 'n' Stuff:

ACCELERATION

The nature of success is surprising.
When it rains, it pours

Two months into my new STEM journey with Mr. Faizan, to say that I was *coming out of my shell* would have been an understatement. Still, I kept the shell close by at all times so that I could scurry back in at a moment's notice.

Standing in front of the class in my best polo shirt, I put a graphic on the fancy new high-def screen (I'd convinced Mr. Faizan to get rid of the projector). It read:

1. Identify and describe the problem clearly.

2. Establish a timeline for the normal situation to the problem's occurrence.

3. Distinguish between the root cause and other factors.

4. Establish a casual graph. (I realized it was supposed to be *causal* graph but enjoyed the vacation vibe of the misspelling.)

"You are all well versed in these steps now." I smacked my hand against my forehead and reminded myself not to pretend that I was Mr. Faizan. I had to pretend to be myself.

Alexis raised her hand. "Mr. Ahmad ..."

"Please don't call me that, bro. That's my dad's name."

"*Hisham*, I have to admit to something."

This could go in any direction. Spring break in Ibiza?

"Yes?"

"I'm not good with the graphs. I find them really hard to make. I don't know—I come up with good inventions, but technology and computers are not my thing."

I turned my attention to Mr. Faizan, who sat at the back of the class. It was the first time I ever saw shock and sheer disgust on his face. He was a computer science major after all.

"Alexis, I totally get it." I pulled up a graph I'd worked on the night before. "This took me five hours."

She shook her head in dismay. "Can't we just have the tech guys do that stuff?"

"No, Alexis. We need to learn all the steps so that we can do everything we need to do ourselves while we don't have money. Then we make money and pay people to do it."

This was a religious moment for Mikhail. "آمين (*Amen*), bro."

His confirmation with an amen reminded me that I had fate on my side. I was going places.

———————————— | MISFIT MOTIVATION | ————————————

I was beginning to understand why Richard Gere
Faizan was still teaching. Teaching others helps you
to grow and develop new skill sets. That super corny
statement is true: "The teacher is also the student."

THE GARDEN OF OUTSIDER CONTEMPLATION

As I sat in the STEM garden eating my shawarma, it occurred to me that I was entirely alone and didn't feel bad about it. I enjoyed a moment of peace with myself. Nothing was perfect yet, but I was coming to grips with being an Outsider, no longer Invisible, until the fucking bluebird appeared overhead and I ran. So much for a moment of tranquility ...

Once the horrible bluebird—synonymous with a pterodactyl of shit in the sky—had disappeared, I returned to the bench and ate my sandwich like a frightened child. What came next was quite unexpected; one by one, the students from STEM entered the garden, and all eyes were on me. They wanted to ... *talk* to me. They had questions. They were in awe. I wished again to be Invisible.

It's one thing to preside over a class as an Outsider teen with Misfit thoughts (and newly Invisible ambitions), but it was another thing altogether to be placed on a pedestal. Popcorn guy, vaguely known as Joseph, sat beside me and reached out his arm onto the back of the bench, gracing my shoulder. This gesture was so uncomfortable that I put down my shawarma and felt a migraine coming.

"Brother, I've been meaning to ask you ..."

Every inch of my body froze. First of all, being called *Brother* was just pure ignorance. I would accept *Bro*, *Dude*, or *Man*, but this was simply uncalled for.

I persevered. "Yes?"

"Like, after the analysis and hypothesis, you experiment with shit and all."

Although I immediately found this conversation annoying, *shit and all* was pretty good, and I'd keep it in my back pocket. "Correct."

"So like, did you experiment with your patent idea before you applied?"

I gave him a dead stare, but deep down, my patent anxiety rose to the surface. I wrote these feelings off by replying. "No, bro. I just knew. The sketch and construction were so strong … that I knew."

Although I spoke with confidence, I still feared imminent failure.

------------------------------ | MISFIT MOTIVATION | ------------------------------

When you're waiting for confirmation on something like a test, school application, or patent approval, it's common for everyone to wonder if they did enough. Did they put in enough hard work? Was there something they missed? Keep in mind that any great thing that you seek to achieve will leave you in a purgatory of your thoughts for a while.

YOUTUBE SCHMUTUBE

Rehan had gained an obsession of late. He wanted me to make more YouTube videos, but I'm pretty sure it was for his own gain. The first video got the attention of girls, and he hoped to dovetail off my success. The dude had literally purchased a GoPro and bought a background.

"Bro, look into the camera."

I shook my head in disgust with my notecard in hand. Surprisingly, my hand didn't shake, and I felt little fear, only the shame of having to upload such crap onto the internet. Without asking, I assumed that Mohammad would agree.

Rehan had gone so far as to also buy a plastic plant for the background. All of this was crazy *Two Ferns*–like to me, and my mortification deepened.

"This is ridiculous, man."

"Come on, Hisham. The girls want to see this," he said with glee.

I looked down at the speech I'd written the night before, half in a daze after creating the same kind of graphic that Alexis complained about. In truth, I hadn't slept much, I didn't figure out that friggin' streetlamp problem, and my eyes were red from fatigue.

"'Kay, then. 'Kay."

Rehan gave me the silent *three, two, one* with his finger, and I jumped in like a car salesman.

"Listen closely: it's time to break free from the chains of regret and poor choices. People spend their entire lives trapped in this cycle, never realizing that the key to breaking free lies in self-discovery. Not knowing who you are is like sailing through life without a compass. It's no wonder that poor choices become the norm."

"Brilliant, bro," Rehan said with crazy eyes as he looked into the screen.

"But I want to inspire you to change that. Take a moment to imagine a future where you know your true essence, your passions, your values, and your purpose. Picture a life where every choice you make aligns with your authentic self. That's the path to true happiness. When you truly know yourself, you gain the power to make choices that nourish your soul and lead you toward a life of fulfillment and joy. Break the cycle, and step into the realm of self-discovery to truly find your purpose."

After Rehan turned the camera off, he swiped away a tear. "That was powerful."

"Really?" I asked, my heart bursting with pride.

He laughed uncontrollably. "Nah, dude. That was so fake."

—————————————— | MISFIT MOTIVATION | ——————————————

Finding your true voice is a theme throughout this book Although I did manage to write this speech, something was off for me What I said was true, but

the Misfit inside us all seeks to speak authentically.
Like with anything else, it takes time and practice

UPS AND DOWNS

As I contemplated Rehan's comment in the privacy of my bedroom, I needed Mr. Kiyosaki more than ever. What if my patent was never approved, I'd never have a girlfriend, and all the hope that Mr. Faizan had placed in me was unfounded? I returned to the seminal book, dog-eared and highlighted.

"Overcoming Obstacles: The primary difference between a rich person and a poor person is how they manage fear."[8]

The main culprits that Kiyosaki suggested for why many aren't financially independent after receiving the proper education were the following:

1. *Fear*

2. *Cynicism*

3. *Laziness*

4. *Bad habits*

5. *Arrogance*[9]

I instantly went to root cause analysis to figure out why all five elements were true for me.

1. *Everything scares the shit out of me*

2. *My patent won't be approved because the system is fucked*

---

8   Kiyosaki, *Rich Dad Poor Dad.*

9   Kiyosaki, *Rich Dad Poor Dad.*

3. *I am **not** lazy.*

4. *Bad habits. Takis, thinking too much about girls, and laziness. Okay ... I was fessing up.*

5. *Give me a sec for some denial ...*

Number five stopped me in my tracks. Was all this attention at STEM and on SchmuTube making me arrogant or something? I didn't think so, but I had to consider it. STEM class treated me like a king, Mr. Faizan went from Obi-Wan to Luke Skywalker, but Mike's Hard Lemonade girl was nowhere in sight. Neither was Maryam ... Even Shirley hadn't knocked on my door.

I put down Mr. Kiyosaki's book, the cover obscured by Marvel stickers, and recalled Joseph's question regarding experimentation with any innovation. It was the action phase—the *scariest* phase because a million things could go wrong. You could be on cloud nine about an idea and have the practical reality of it blow up in your face.

I decided to work on problem analysis at this very moment, define the factors, and enact experimentation. I wrote it all down on my steno pad while also sketching those weird samurai swords again.

IMPOSTER SYNDROME ROOT CAUSE ANALYSIS

I have imposter syndrome because people are starting to look at me. I'm not as Invisible. Rehan has this weird habit of uploading me on YouTube. None of this makes sense because I'm an Outsider. Even Soraya is being nice to me because I've proved myself to her. The librarian winks at me in the halls. I believe that this imposter syndrome comes from such a rapid change in a small space of time, and the Misfit inside me would rather pick and choose who I get attention from.

Weakest Link: People are paying attention to me because they like me.

Wild Idea Brainstorming:

1. *Rehan is using me to eventually get laid*

2. *Soraya wants to make money off of me and move to Dubai with Faizan and Dad*

3. *Librarian had a crush on me all along*

4. *I'm not, in fact, Invisible*

Hypothesis: There's a very good chance that I have more potential than I realized.

I instantly called Mr. Faizan with my results.

EXPERIMENTATION

It was like we were in an Edward Hopper painting, seated in a mysterious diner late at night. Outside, the streets were quiet. One lone waitress made a fresh pot of coffee, and I pushed around a pancake dinner with my fork. Okay, it wasn't a moody diner; it was the International House of Pancakes. Mr. Faizan had a thing for IHOP, and I never complained.

"I'm seeing changes in you, Hisham." He ate an omelet, which was certainly the reason he was more ripped than I was.

"I'm not feeling it, though. It's like … an out-of-body experience. People are paying more attention to me, but I keep asking why."

"It's because you have so much to *give*. I saw it immediately, and that's why I asked you to take more ownership of STEM."

I watched the butter coagulate with the maple syrup and became lost in thought. "What if this goes nowhere? What if I just end up as a STEM teacher like you?"

Mr. Faizan gave me a grave look. "I invent for NASA, and I am a millionaire."

"Right, cool. I forgot."

"You're accelerating your life at a marvelous pace, Hisham. Your whole life is ahead of you." He squirted ketchup onto his eggs, and I cringed. "Remember what I told you about patience? Confidence will *also* take some patience. It will come ..."

I gave a heavy sigh like a brooding lover. "Maryam still doesn't pay attention to me. Maybe the whole world will eventually pay attention to me but not her."

"That's because you don't stand a chance, Hisham."

"Bro?"

He shook his head. "You don't stand a chance. You can invent real-world innovations, but you can't invent attraction."

I was beet red with fury. No, no, I'd find a way! It was unethical as all hell, but I'd find a way ... "Dude, I'm familiar with electroencephalography. The mind can control things."

"Not someone else's mind."

"Shit, I didn't think of that."

"Because, as you know from patent law, such technology would be dangerous and therefore is unable to bring to reality."

Mr. Faizan was on his game. No, it would be unethical to control Maryam's mind, and as soon as I was no longer a teenager, I'd realize that.

"So what do I do, bro? It's driving me insane!" Maybe it was misplaced patent anxiety, but I truly had to wonder if any girl would ever like me. Mikhail liked me and popcorn guy. Rehan did spend time with me (but used me for my Nintendo), and even Mountain Dew guy now gave me a respectful lift of the chin from afar. However, Alexis was the only girl who looked at me fondly. "I want to score with Maryam!"

141

Mr. Faizan gave me an admonishing stare. "You can't. The Quran clearly states that premarital sex is forbidden."

I jabbed my fork into my pancakes, prompting the utensil to stand up straight. "Speak English, bro."

"I mean that you can't get laid."

It was the most honest thing Mr. Faizan had ever said to me.

───── | MISFIT MOTIVATION | ─────

I have no comment about this section

THE FUNK

I told Mr. Faizan that I wanted to walk home from IHOP. I needed to clear my head. Each streetlamp taunted me, reminding me that my inventions were crap and my life was going nowhere. Cars passed by, their headlights in my face. Even that pissed me off. Why hadn't anyone invented headlights that proved effective but not blinding?

Sure, there were halogen lights, but most consumers wouldn't buy these. Why?

1. *They're more expensive*

2. *Most drivers don't want to replace their bulbs unless they must*

3. *They don't last as long*

4. *People are assholes*

Radiohead's "Creep" played in my mind as I continued along, feeling more like an Outsider than ever before.

Mr. Faizan's car pulled up beside me. "Hisham, this is ridiculous. Get in the car."

"Let me have my moment."

"Get in the car."

Yes, my walk of IHOP shame had been briefly pathetic, so I guess that I was wallowing. I wanted to delay going home and prepping for the STEM curriculum tomorrow. Don't get me wrong—I loved teaching; I was just in a funk.

Mr. Faizan gripped the wheel of the car with urgency. "We must act fast. Your father called me."

A cold wave of worry ran up my spine. "What did he say?"

"We have to wait. Buckle your seat belt."

Cue the awesome Mafia shit! This was getting good. Something was up, and the situation was turning into a *Fast & Furious* scene in Faizan's Hyundai Accord. How this guy was a millionaire and didn't have a Lambo, I have no idea. But Mr. Kiyosaki would agree that a fancy car is not an asset, and neither is a home for that matter.

Stopped at a red light, I said, "Bro, you gotta get a new car."

"This is very functional, Hisham."

"It won't get you the ladies."

"I don't need the ladies. I'm married."

"Good point."

Just as the light went green, Mr. Faizan sped ahead, and I watched the suburban streets of Dallas whiz past. We stopped again as a pedestrian crossed the sidewalk, followed by another. We accelerated once more, then stopped behind what I call a عربة الجدة (grandma vehicle). Lastly, someone rode a bike—*a bike*—in the middle of the street. This was turning into the most pathetic chase one could ever witness.

I resigned myself to the moment but stood resolute. "Bro, this is why I'm getting a Lambo. People will get out of the way."

A FUTURE FLEX

As I stepped into my home, I was prepared for anything.

Problem analysis:

1. *My dad was sick.*

2. *I was being scolded for going to IHOP.*

3. *The dog died.*

4. *Maryam had called and left a message, and my dad was*
   pissed that I was attempting to talk to girls.

When he stepped out of his office, the warm campfire of his desktop emanating comfort, I was surprised by his lighthearted tone. "Hisham, we have wonderful news."

I replied with complete sincerity, "There's a new passage in the Quran that says I can have a girl before marriage?"

I heard Mr. Faizan smack his forehead.

My dad remained resolute. "No, son. Far more important."

I didn't know what could have been more important, but as he handed me the open envelope from the USPTO, I suddenly knew. I pulled the certificate out, witnessing the gold seal of approval.

"You did it, Hisham," my father said with pride. "Within months. It's so very rare."

Mr. Faizan came in for a hug, and I let it happen but had to give that awkward dude *pat on the back*. Like, you had to make it loud to be more manly. As Mr. Faizan pulled away, genuine emotion hit me hard.

When a tear fell (far more difficult to show vulnerability in front of older dudes), I let it happen. I was so very happy.

"I can't believe it. I thought that I had to wait years," I admitted, pulling an IHOP napkin from my pocket.

My father spoke candidly. "Hisham, this is the beginning of many triumphs. I know it, and Mr. Faizan knows it. This is *only* the beginning."

With this first certificate, something shifted in me. Being an Outsider and Invisible no longer mattered. I had received confirmation of a sincere purpose inside me. I'd do the unthinkable. Hisham Ahmad would go from Misfit to Mogul.

Life is about identifying problems, coming up with solutions, testing those solutions, and eventually experimenting with what you came up with. You can skip the problem statement and hypothesis because that's the boring shit. But this method can be applied to anything. Ultimately, it's about taking action. The work that you put in will bring you to a conclusion, and then you must test things. This is also known as "grabbing the bull by its horns." That sounds dangerous, so don't do that with a real bull.

I quickly received my first patent because I'd gone through the laborious process that STEM taught me. I was learning about law and finance mostly for the sake of Shirley. When I wrote that speech that I low-key hate, I meant it when it comes to the importance of self-discovery. This kind of work takes you out of your shell and helps you to collaborate with others. You truly can go from Misfit to Mogul, but you can't do it alone.

In the last section of this book, I'm gonna flex a bit. The point of it all is that I quickly began to live my dream. This isn't out of reach for you. All you need are the proper tools, and as the great Kiyosaki said, "There is gold everywhere. Most people are not trained to see it."[10] Well, this Invisible Outsider started to see gold.

Invisible Homework

- You can come up with a ton of answers to a problem, but experimentation is key. Look at your major problem and the various solutions. Experiment with each of these.

---

10   Kiyosaki, *Rich Dad Poor Dad.*

- Experimentation takes the onus off the solution. Say your problem is that you're too skinny, and you try a ton of things to get bigger (there's nothing wrong with being skinny BTW), and through your experimentation, you find what works for you. When something doesn't work, it's not your fault. You tried. Write down the things you want to experiment with this week.

Notes 'n' Stuff:

9

LAUNCH

Launching to success is a calculated choice that comes from hard work, determination, and Outsider thinking.

Rehan diligently held his GoPro as I huffed in despair. This was getting old, and I would have rather watched him play Nintendo with his dirty Doritos fingers. Still, I was in the habit of practicing my writing and speaking, which, after I'd taught STEM for one year, had gotten quite good. After becoming a partial owner of STEM, I'd been awarded two other patents and explored business ventures with Mr. Faizan. But with all this glory came no girlfriend …

"I'm ready for you, bro," Rehan said, looking into the camera.

"Dude, that's a camera for action films. I'm not gonna snowboard down a mountain or something. I'm not gonna set something on fire."

"I need you to *bring* your fire." He looked me square in the face. "Do it for the kids."

This was pathetic, but you know what I say about pushing your boundaries and practicing. Off I went, speaking to the kids. "Why does every problem have only one correct answer? I mean, I could be looking at a six, and you could be looking at a nine. I could be seeing a glass half-full, and you could be seeing a glass half-empty. You get the point."

"Good point, bro."

I wasn't sure how he'd edit out that interruption, but Rehan had done so in the past. I continued. "When I'm taking a test at school, there's only one right answer. Why are we constantly limiting students' creativity and living under the fear of 'when will we make a mistake, or when will we be wrong'? Being wrong is *subjective*. Shit—I'm sorry. I meant *heck*. Edit that out, Rehan."

"No way, man."

"Shit, a lot of successful entrepreneurs were 'wrong' time and time again before getting it right. Making mistakes and failing is what grants you the experience and exposure to be successful. It's not wrong to be wrong!"

Feeling vulnerable, I looked at Rehan for confirmation. "Keep going, keep going. Talk about personal stuff, bro."

"Why the fuck?"

"Your followers want to hear it. Tell them about the Natalies."

I gave him a blank stare. "No."

| MISFIT MOTIVATION |

Content creation is important. Perhaps all that you want to do is draw and invent, solve real-world problems, and make a fortune, but considering the times that we live in, you'll have to learn about social media. Pro tip: you can use it professionally but avoid it personally.

THE NATALIES OF THE WORLD

It was true that I had become popular with a few different Natalies after growing some confidence and success. They were very nice girls but not my cup of tea. Maryam was still my espresso.

As I stood in front of STEM class, using my old-man red laser light to bring attention to the screen, I feared that my youth was lost at sixteen (I was not, however, wearing crocs and socks … not yet). There was some added comfort when Natalie number one stared at me in awe, and Alexis gave Natalie a side glance of jealous daggers.

"Step ten," I said. "Ask yourself: What part of this innovation will be the reason we get the patent? Does the solution already exist? Can we find evidence of it *anywhere* online? Is the solution useful? Is our invention nonobvious? Meaning, would this be one of the first things someone thinks of when they consider an innovation to the problem?"

Natalie raised her hand, and my attention was brought to her fake fingernails and cute rings that she no doubt bought at the mall. "Mr. Ahmad?"

"That is my father's name. Please."

"Hisham," she corrected herself, fluttering her lashes. "How many patents do you have now?"

The honest answer was three, but I had ten more down the pipeline. Still, I felt the need to keep the topic on point. Being a partial owner of STEM, I had to pretend to be an adult. "That is irrelevant, Natalie. This process that I've outlined could lead to several patents or just one *important* one. It's about quality and not quantity." Except for when it came to all the cars that I wanted.

"As you said … it's okay to be wrong."

Yep. Confirmation. Natalie was stalking me.

"It's better to get it right once than overtax yourself, getting multiple things right. Put your focus into one problem and go through all the steps outlined here." Old-man red laser light was pointed again.

"But really …" She was coaxing me, turning her hip to the side. I knew exactly what was happening, and my teenage brain was melting. "Are you gonna be a millionaire or something?"

Dry mouthed, I looked to Mr. Faizan at the back of the class, desperately seeking the right response. He appeared very annoyed by the question, so I replied with an annoying answer, "Yes, Natalie. I will be."

———————— | MISFIT MOTIVATION | ————————

Sometimes, you fully see the outcome that you seek. You have big dreams and you say yes to them, even if it sounds crazy. It's the Shirleys of the world who act as cheerleaders when trying to achieve what others deem impossible.

THE REALITY OF REAL ESTATE

Later that day, I rode my bike from STEM to Bluffview for the showing of a mansion for sale. On the way, I stopped at a boba tea shop and secretly hoped I wouldn't encounter Natalie number two. Sure enough, she was behind the counter wearing an Aerosmith T-shirt, which for a brown girl of her age could just be chalked up to irony.

"Hey, Hisham. I watched your YouTube video," she cooed.

In my mind, I was cursing Rehan! Why was he putting me through this Outsider early-life social media crisis?

"Hey, dude."

It goes without saying that a greeting of dude is not gender specific.

"The usual?" she asked.

"Yeah. Thanks, bro."

As she worked on my tea, I couldn't help but wonder if girls could smell future success. I mean, not like I didn't intend for this phenomenon to happen, but Natalie number two wasn't the exquisite creature that I wanted. Although I could make her my girlfriend if I felt like it (culturally, I still couldn't go any further), I had to wonder if it was *me* that she liked or my growing wallet. This conundrum would continue in the future …

"Here you go, Hisham," she said, handing over my brown sugar milk tea.

"Thank you, Natalie number two," I replied before leaving the shop.

It was a twenty-minute ride to the community of Bluffview. As I rode past the palatial houses, my eyebrows shot up. Feeling out of place was only made more embarrassing by pedaling while sipping from a boba tea. I had been practicing my Misfit Mogul face and used it now, imitating the eye of the tiger.

Once I spotted my father's car in front of a particularly beautiful mansion, I kept speeding ahead until I saw the real estate agent with massive real estate of her own (pardon me, I'm a teenage kid) walk outside and wave to me in a blue dress suit. The image was so jarring that I fell from my bike and spilled my tea. This event luckily happened on a fluffy green lawn.

As she ran toward me, there were only two things I paid attention to.

"You must be Hisham! Are you okay?"

"I'm fine. I think I hit a"—I was respectfully making it up on the fly—"curb, or something."

My father joined the real estate agent, and then my mortification was complete. "Son, what has happened?"

"I got"—gulp—"distracted." Please, Allah, make me eighteen soon.

———————— | MISFIT MOTIVATION | ————————

Most real estate agents are hot, no matter
their age. You just have to wait to get
older in this kind of situation.

THE DAD-ING OF AMERICA

I managed to dust myself off, but the grass stains on my polo shirt still clearly presented my failure. All of this shame drifted away as I walked through the palatial estate, the real estate agent known as (no joke) Natalie number three walking my father and me through the five-bedroom, five-bath property with a fancy pool in the expansive yard.

"This gated community is highly sought after," Natalie number three said as she strutted along. "This marvelous home boasts of an open-concept design, modern appliances, and a stunning backyard. Thanks to the open-concept plan, there is an effortless flow from the kitchen, dining areas, and living room," she said as her high heels clicked on the marble floor.

"This is fantastic, Natalie," my father replied, walking along with his hands clasped behind his back.

"The backyard is a peaceful oasis, perfect for entertaining and enjoying summer evenings in the pool or beside the fire," she said with a grin. "Let me know if you have any questions, Mr. Ahmad," she added, putting out her glittering hand for a shake.

My father grasped her hand and replied, "That is all for now, Natalie number three." I shot my father a look. Yes, he could read my mind, and the realization was terrifying. "Allow me a moment alone with my son."

As Natalie number three pulled open the effortless sliding glass door to the yard, I stepped outside with my dad, buzzing with a million questions. The water of the large pool glimmered with the light of the sun, and, thank you, Allah, there were no bluebirds.

"Why did you want me to see this?" I asked.

My father, in his placid wisdom, supplied a concrete answer. "I want you to begin to invest in real estate."

As a partial owner of STEM, I wasn't sure how I'd be able to afford something like this, and I recalled from *Rich Dad Poor Dad* that I might piss Mr. Kiyosaki off because this palace wasn't an asset. My father proved me wrong.

I gave my best son-like response. "Sure, cool. Um … why?"

"What we're doing is building your future. You don't have to know everything about each topic; you just have to know enough about each issue to build your portfolio and build your passive income to live a life of prosperity. Real estate comes into play. As your income is growing, investment in real estate means that you can rent this property out for nearly fourteen thousand dollars a month. Then, you can invest in another property and do the same. This passive income will allow you to focus on your innovations, patents, and future business prospects."

"I don't have the cash."

"You have plenty of cash, son. And I will help, as well."

If Mr. Faizan was Obi-Wan, my dad was turning into a benevolent Darth Vader. "So it's true? You do want me to become rich so that you can move to Dubai."

My father dad-ed me with a look of frustration. "No, son. This is how you build generational wealth … for your children and my grandchildren."

"Cool. Awesome." I was completely on board because surely my dad was implying that I'd marry Maryam one day and make a ton of kids.

| MISFIT MOTIVATION |

Although real estate isn't considered an asset, purchasing it early in life will lead to multiple opportunities to one day retire in Margaritaville More importantly, this effort will afford you more time to focus on your Misfit/Outsider ideas and creations.

MISFITS OF THE FUTURE

It was several months later that I stood in the very same mansion, staring into Rehan's GoPro with two *real* plants behind me. This time, there was no fake backdrop like the one that had looked like it was stolen from a high school yearbook photographer. What surrounded me now was an opulent home, and through the window, pristine surroundings that yelled "I'm rich!"

My speech for today had been written in the middle of the night while I was suffering from a nosebleed. "It's often said that 'children are the future,' but how can you expect us to be the future when the current school system is still in the past? I mean, we spend over a decade at what should be *preparing* us for the future, yet it's untrue. Not even for something as simple as college, let alone being an entrepreneur."

Rehan made his customary, inappropriate comment while looking at the high ceilings in awe. "Bro, you're rich. What the hell?"

I wasn't exactly rich, but I was investing as my father had instructed me to do.

Clearing my throat several times after this distraction, I continued. "We should have all the resources to be creative, driven, and passionate when it comes to following our dreams—not continuously limited to following instructions. I believe in order for students to change the future, we must make changes to the foundation built by the education system. We must see innovation rise at an exponential rate. Listen, if you want to see big changes, then *make* big changes!"

Once my speech was done, I looked to Rehan for encouragement as he shook his head in disgust. "Nah, bro. Now say what you really mean. Like you're talking to Maryam … Three, two, one. Go!"

Even though Rehan always busted my balls, he managed to get the truth out of me.

"Okay, I'm working on my speeches, guys. I always say the right things, and I mean what I say. But I guess I'll just add to it. I'm in a crazy-ass mansion now, and yeah, I own it. This isn't to show off or anything, but I'm starting to invest my money at, like, a young age. And then it grows. This is the shit you're not taught, and no one encourages you to do so. There's a stigma against wealth, and that keeps you poor."

Rehan was overly excited. "Keep going!"

"First of all, don't judge wealth or anyone else with wealth. Then, *decide* that you want it, you know? Like the great Kiyosaki says in *Rich Dad Poor Dad*." I pulled the book from my back pocket like every Outsider with a pocket protector must do.

"Smooth, bro. Smooth."

I read from the seminal book. "'Becoming rich wasn't easy, but it wasn't that hard either.'[11] The meaning behind that quote is that you have to want something and know your *purpose* behind wanting that great thing. I began to innovate because my mind was crazy with ideas. I had mentors who guided me along the way, and now I'm just gonna get fucking rich."

Rehan, stricken, quickly switched off the camera.

"Too much?" I asked.

"Nah, dude." He swiped away a tear. "You're so getting laid soon."

| MISFIT MOTIVATION |

*Find those books in life that are so inspiring and spot-on that you keep them in your back pocket at all times. As I read from **Rich Dad Poor Dad** I'm sure that Rehan was clutching the Quran. Off in a distant place, Shirley might have held the **Guide to Taxation** Outsiders must always carry books, and preferably, not your math book from school.*

----

11   Kiyosaki, *Rich Dad Poor Dad*.

RIDICULOUS ABANDON

Things got real. After the YouTube video was edited and uploaded, Rehan and I lost our minds. We ran around the house and went insane. "Dude, I can't believe you own this!"

"It's crazy!" I screamed, bouncing up and down on a king-size bed.

The scene was like a house party for two, but without the alcohol or beautiful girls. Just imagine: cans of Coke strewn everywhere, bags of Doritos hanging from the chandeliers, and empty boxes of pizza used as sleds to ride down the stairs.

"This life is fucking *awesome*!" Rehan screamed like an animal.

I ran out to the pool with my out-of-his-mind friend following me. Climbing onto one of the rock waterfall cliffs, I ripped off my shirt and proclaimed, "I'm the king of the world!" I dove in like a pro, feeling the cold water envelop my skin and basking in one of the most exciting and thrilling Outsider moments of my life.

Sinking to the bottom of the pool, I looked up at the billowing surface of the water and noticed not one person standing there, but two. I was in trouble for something. I just knew it. The Misfit that had been dying to come out was literally and figuratively rising to the surface.

As I crested the top of the water, I discovered Mr. Faizan standing there, his arms crossed in front of his chest. Trying to brush off the temporary insanity, I transitioned into a gentle backstroke that I knew Faizan would find acceptable.

"Hisham, you missed the meeting today."

As I had a panic attack in a pool no less grand than that of Hearst Castle, I managed to remain perfectly calm. "No way. I totally forgot. That's weird."

When I looked to Rehan in sheer terror, he pointed to his nose, giving me the tried and true bro signal. I noticed the blood coming down my chest. My nose always spoke louder than words.

You can put your energy into becoming an entrepreneur and game changer, but sometimes you have to let loose

STEM CONFERENCE ROOM PUKE FEST

Neurosurgeon Abdul Baker sat with Mr. Faizan and me in his fancy conference room, a massive framed picture of Dubai behind him. The room was definitely nicer than ours at the STEM warehouse, and I already had a plan in place to make our room look better than something out of *The Office*.

"Hisham, I've seen your sketches for the exoskeleton, and I'm quite impressed. So is the crown prince's brother."

"Which one?" I asked, knowing there were six.

He answered, "لادن الجزير لورنس العرب عبد الفريد عظيم بن".

Surely, my mind was playing tricks on me because all that I heard was *Lawrence of Arabia Abdul Fareed Azim bin Laden Al Jazeer*.

Nonetheless, it would be very difficult to admit during this conversation the truth behind my innovation. The exoskeleton idea was meant to help me out of bed in the morning, but more importantly, to assist those with disabilities that weren't solely fatigue oriented.

I had to hold it together. "It is cool to finally meet you," I managed to say, bringing a napkin to my nose.

"I want to develop this idea with both you and Mr. Faizan. I think this innovation will help many. أنت شاب ذكي."

Oh god … oh god … my Arabic sucked. My father insisted I take classes, but with everything else going on, I much preferred to run around my new mansion like an unhinged Misfit.

There were three options for what Mr. Baker had said:

1. You're a skinny young man.

2. You're a loser young man.

3. You're a smart young man.

I clung to hope and went with option number three.

"Speak, Hisham," Mr. Faizan whispered.

Damn it. Here we go. "انه لطف منك .ٌشكرأ جزيلا." Essentially, *Shkraan jzylaan. anah lutif minka. (Thank you very much. That is kind of you.)*

Mr. Baker appeared pleased with my response, and I experienced a wave of relief, determined to double down on my Arabic lessons. He continued, "I hear that you already have several patents now. Let us meet once a week to bring this project to life."

"Yes, sir. I ... think this idea is GOAT."

Only in my imagination did I hear Mr. Faizan smack his forehead.

"Very well. Till next time," Mr. Baker said.

Once the call was done, I heaved a sigh of relief and turned to Mr. Faizan. "Will he give me a Lambo?"

He grinned from ear to ear. "Hisham, your father wants you to invest in a second property. You partially own a business, and we're creating another ... You can buy one for yourself."

Through my utter excitement and elation, I spoke those two profound Outsider words: "Okay, lit."

—————— | MISFIT MOTIVATION | ——————

"Okay, lit" is a perfectly reasonable response to anything.

Success happens fast when you've built the infrastructure for it, and as I shared from Mr. Kiyosaki's quote, you also have a reason *why* you want to be successful. Sure, I wanted to be rich and powerful, but there was something more important that drove me: I wanted to do the unthinkable. I wanted to prove to others that life doesn't have to follow the normal trajectory that we all expect. We can all reach higher and at a young age.

I will admit that as the money rolled in, the Misfit inside grew louder. The Outsider still grappled with not being seen in the way that he wanted. I was respected in STEM and now on a sorta global level (as well as by the hot real estate lady), but there was a missing piece.

The teenage Misfit within was being seen for his accomplishments and crazy imagination, but not for who he was. That's me getting all *self-help*, but it's a true phenomenon. Everything "nonconventional" that I was learning (although incredibly conventional, just ahead of my time) propelled me into the world. That world was still scary.

I could have retreated into introspection and yoga. I could have sent Maryam flowers and written a kind note about how beautiful her soul is. I could have learned better Arabic and opened a mega-Mosque, preaching to my people as I preached in STEM.

Instead, I let the Misfit come out in all his glory. The Outsider was enjoying his payday, and much work went into making it happen.

Invisible Homework

Owning your triumphs is incredibly hard for the Outsider. It's difficult to accept a win when your brain is hardwired to be

Invisible. Remember what Mr. Kiyosaki said: "Without a strong reason or purpose, everything in life is hard."[12]

- *There's a stigma against being rich, and that's just absolute bullshit. On the next page, write your reasons for wanting to become rich. Lambos and girls are totally legitimate, but keep digging to find a deeper purpose: something that others benefit from.*

---

12   Kiyosaki, *Rich Dad Poor Dad*.

Notes 'n' Stuff:

THE POWER OF BLING

*Use intention or sheer Misfit determination to
receive bling. Your choices, habits, and routines
need to be calculated or plainly insane.*

Standing at the Lamborghini dealership in Dallas was a dream come true. Dad had tried to convince me to purchase a Volvo, but there was a deeper meaning behind this luxury acquisition. Sure, it was no investment. The thing would perhaps cost a fortune to maintain, but I *wanted* it. Dreamt about it. And I, of course, hoped it would help me to get the girl.

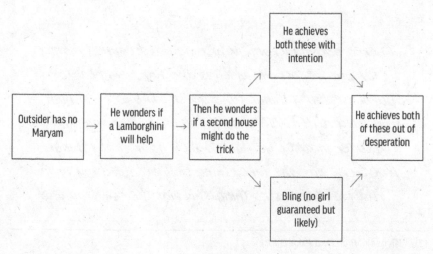

It was only on my seventeenth birthday that I could make this dream happen. Even though my father wouldn't allow me to have a cell phone, he agreed to the Lambo. Why? Because I'd worked hard and earned the money.

As I sat in the leather chair across the desk from the salesman, I pulled out *Rich Dad Poor Dad*, if only for encouragement. I'd been diligently working on the Study Sessions at the back of the book, and one question jumped out at me: "The last time you purchased a luxury, how did you pay for it?"[13]

The timing was just right for the salesman with the retro 'stache to ask, "Mr. Ahmad, how would you like to pay?"

I cleared my throat. "Um, that's my dad's name. But … I'll pay on a credit card."

Okay, Mr. Kiyosaki was perhaps judging me from afar, but I'd done the accounting. I knew that I could afford the Lambo in cash. I thought it fitting to use my free assets in places where the money would grow while the Lambo was being paid off on the card. The income from my two properties gave me a tremendous amount of leverage. Everything was growing at the same time, and with all that I'd learned so far, it was time for bling.

───── | MISFIT MOTIVATION | ─────

*There's nothing wrong with using hard-earned money (or passive income, which is also hard earned) to purchase fancy things. Who doesn't like to have high-quality stuff? With enough intention, learning, and Outsider insanity, you get to pick your fancy things. But there was one fancy thing that occupied my mind. Trust me: this was no **thing**; this was the الهة (Goddess!*

13 Kiyosaki, *Rich Dad Poor Dad*.

OUTSIDER TEST-DRIVING

As Rehan and I took our first cruise in the red Lambo I'd named Ice Man, I watched while he perilously grasped a can of Dr Pepper and his bag of Doritos. As crumbs spilled into my car's pristine new green interior and the soda appeared to almost spill, I dad-ed him hard.

"Bro, you cannot eat or drink in this car!"

"Bro, what's the big deal?" he asked, licking his finger.

Oh, god. I was disgusted. I made a vow: from here on out, only girls could ride shotgun. No Natalies, though.

"You're messing up my ride!" I protested, scowling at him.

"Dude, watch where you're going!"

I returned my attention to the road, seeing that the car ahead of me had made an abrupt stop. Slamming on the brakes, I put my hand in front of Rehan, giving him the mom arm. Once we were safely stopped, I looked down to discover Dr Pepper all over my green leather seats.

Rehan was stricken. "I'm sorry, man. I didn't know you'd stop so fast."

My eyes flung daggers at him. All I could do was shake my head in fury and continue driving.

When we pulled into the high school parking lot, I watched as students turned in awe. The Misfit in me smiled, the Invisible kid burst with pride, but the Outsider had a moment of panic. Sure, the Lambo gave me attention, but it was the hard work that I wanted attention for. I had the bling but deeply craved respect.

Once we parked, I released the doors, which rose into the sky like the DeLorean's from *Back to the Future*. I should have hired someone to execute the fog effect. Off in the distance, I saw the rack where I used to store my bike, and just beside it stood Maryam, looking as glorious as always. She wore a green hijab that day. It would work well with Ice Man's majestic rain forest interior. This was fate, I reasoned.

Rehan noticed my piqued interest and said, "Dude, no. She has no personality."

"I will cut you," I replied. It was a vicious Pakistani *West Side Story* moment.

He put up his hands in submission. "Okay, okay. I won't say anything more."

As I watched her dress billowing in the wind, I grew introspective. I thought of Mr. Kiyosaki's sentiment: wanting things but having a deep reason behind working for what you want. Not being afraid of wanting luxury and opulence.

As I lowered the doors to my new Lamborghini, I considered that desire for beautiful things was in no way wrong if you had *earned* them. Sadly, I hadn't earned Maryam. She glanced at my Lambo and walked away.

─────────── | MISFIT MOTIVATION | ───────────

*Bling is fun, and contrary to popular belief, it does make you feel happy. But, Outsider Bros, you know you need more. You want to be respected for your achievements. You want people to truly see you. Bling makes you feel seen, but it's important to surround yourself with people who see the **real** you. If you have no idea who you are yet, that's lit too. It will come into perspective as you continue to buy random shit and have people randomly stare at you.*

TUPPERWARE GODS

Rehan and I had transcended to a new level. Whether it was because of the Lambo or due to every other achievement I was enjoying, we now sat in the cafeteria ... eating pizza.

Soda-throwing guy actually got up from his table (abandoning the other jocks) and paid homage.

"Yo, brother. That car is sick," he commented.

Yet again, the full use of the word *brother* felt wildly uncouth.

"Thanks, bro. Got it today."

Soda guy was nervously sweating, and I had to wonder if deep down he was an Outsider as well. "Like, I always wanted one of those. I'll never afford it."

Although this was a tremendous moment of retribution and justice, I couldn't help but turn introspective again. Why didn't Mountain Dew guy think that he could ever afford it? Was he only following what we learned in this terrible school? Did his parents work in cubicles (no shame, we need these folks), and so he thought there was nothing better for him? Although my success of late had been fast and strange, I literally wanted to help out this guy who had bullied me.

I reached into my backpack and pulled out the Quran of financial success. When I flashed him the cover, he appeared confused.

"What's that, brother?"

Oh, right. I remembered that *Rich Dad Poor Dad* had been covered in stickers to conceal my Outsider ambition.

"It's just a book, bro. I got it from the library. It teaches you important shit."

Mountain Dew guy brought a fist to his lips and grinned. "Dude, you took the book and put like Superman and shit on it?"

I had a sinking feeling … Yes, it was true. I'd stolen the book from the library at the beginning of my journey to becoming a Misfit Mogul. I would make it up to library lady … I'd order a fresh copy and have it delivered to my patented lockbox. I'd also order markers for Maryam. It was merely a matter of getting on to Dad's computer to access Amazon.

Becoming rich is weird. You'll make friends you didn't know you had. Please, please make sure these are real friends with good intentions. People can be assholes, and then they're all of a sudden nice because they want your bling. Thank God I met Rehan when I was Invisible نعمة ولعنة (A blessing and a curse)

THE ROOM WHERE IT HAPPENS (BLATANT HAMILTON REFERENCE)

As I projected a problem onto the STEM screen, I realized that I'd mastered my robot voice.

"Problem: Fifty-seven percent of all pencils are mechanical pencils. Mechanical pencils can be refilled with new lead after all the lead is used up. You can typically put three to five sticks of lead in the pencil. A single lead can last one to two days on average. If you put in the max amount of five sticks, the lead can last up to ten days. Because mechanical pencil lead is very thin, it breaks easily, which could reduce the life of the lead. This project aims to develop a better mechanical pencil that decreases the probability of lead breaking."

"What a ginormous problem!" Alexis nearly screamed.

"Indeed. Take a look at this graph."

Mikhail offered a profound reply. "Dude, this is boring." He swiftly perked up. "So, when did you get the Lamborghini?"

The class broke into laughter, and I found myself getting all Dad again. "I purchased the vehicle this morning, but it came from understanding *these* principles." I pointed to the flowchart and used my best Mr. Faizan voice. "This kind of problem-solving is the basis for how I purchased my Lambo."

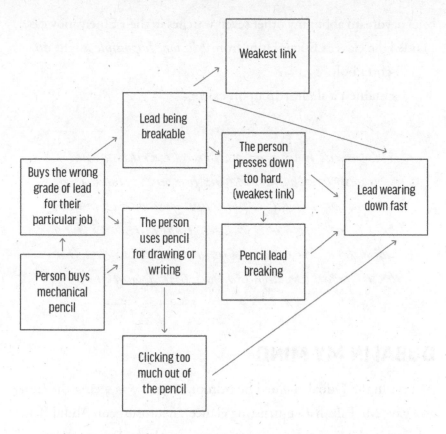

"Give the deets, brother. This is driving me crazy," popcorn guy said.

It was my first Tony Robbins moment. Perhaps the impromptu speech was over the top, but I began to have a new view of things.

"You have to have that drive, bro. We can all achieve the same things. Everyone in this classroom is smart; we just have to learn the skills and be clear about what we want to achieve. Honestly, it's hard and it's not hard. You need the proper mentality. So many people say that *the sky's the limit*. It's actually true. You must have a deep purpose behind what you want."

I stood there as a humble Outsider, finding the greater meaning in what compels us to be innovators, help others, and even earn some bling during the process. As I checked my Rolex Submariner (and had a

brief daydream about my other seven watches in their Emelyanov case),
I ended the class as Ethan Hunt from *Mission: Impossible* might do.

"I gotta bolt."

I sustained a slight trip upon exiting.

| MISFIT MOTIVATION |

*You must have purpose behind everything that
you wish to achieve Find the purpose behind your
innovation, behind a connection you wish to make,
or a hurdle you wish to jump Find purpose behind
your drive for bling and your financial future If it
doesn't mean something to you, then it won't happen*

DUBAI IN MY MIND

As I sat in the Dubai-themed boardroom (yes, I was seeing the irony
and gave Mr. Faizan an untrusting glance), neurosurgeon Abdul Baker
ushered in the first incarnation of our exoskeleton in action.

"What do you think, Hisham?"

I scratched my chin. There were a hundred things that came to
mind, but I pinpointed five of them while keeping it to myself.

1. *The exoskeleton is too bulky*

2. *The "test driver" man appeared unstable, as though he might fall*

3. *The device was too expensive to produce*

4. *Other exoskeletons on the market could compete*

5. *Mr. Faizan would be pissed if this wasn't the best of the best*

"I think there are some changes that we can make," I diplomatically replied. "I just see some stuff that, like, could be better."

Mr. Faizan admonished me like a mother of a two-year-old. "Hisham, use your words."

God, this guy … he hadn't bought me ice cream in weeks.

"Mr. Baker, I feel as though the construction needs improvement. Would this device be helpful for those in need? Yes, but other patents already surpass this, including that from the University of Washington. If we want to compete, we must look at how what we're doing sets us apart and solves problems that the latest patents can't solve."

"That is a wise thing to say, Hisham," Mr. Baker replied.

"And like seriously, though." I continued to watch the poor dude in the exoskeleton that wouldn't stop moving. "Like, get him a beer or something. That looks rough."

As I said this, the exoskeleton slammed into a wall and stopped moving altogether. The passenger just stood there silently …

"The crown prince's brother has offered additional funds for us to continue to innovate this design. I'm confident that your bright young brain will make it happen."

Bright young brain made me think of Frankenstein or something creepy like that. "Cool."

I marveled at the aquamarine-and-turquoise photo of Dubai. There had to be some kind of *Star Trek* invention that would take me there immediately without anyone knowing, my avatar stepping in and dealing with the adults here in Texas.

Abdul noticed my interest. "I do hope that you visit Dubai one day. This is where I am from."

You guys, this Dubai conspiracy theory shit was getting real.

More importantly, I thought of those pristine blue seas and felt like I was going somewhere, even if only within myself. Things were beginning to fall into place in terms of the nexus between innovation, changing the world, success, and, ultimately, bling.

You could say that innovation is a game to make money, but I began to realize that it was much more about the unrelenting, insatiable game of doing what humanity has done throughout history—making shit better. In a capitalistic society, that brings the bling, but what's far more important? An Outsider putting their stamp on the world and moving it a few inches forward.

"Hisham, let's meet again in a few days," Mr. Baker said with satisfaction. "In the meantime, continue with your sketches. We shall figure this out together."

"I know that we will, sir."

"Please," he said with a bow, "call me Abdul."

I was far too quick to reply, "Kareem Abdul-Jabbar."

Mr. Faizan silently shook his head in shame.

"I'm sorry?" Mr. Baker asked.

"I apologize. The name Abdul always makes me think of basketball."

—————— | MISFIT MOTIVATION | ——————

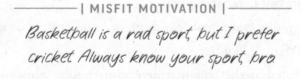

Basketball is a rad sport, but I prefer cricket. Always know your sport, bro.

REAL ESTATE SNOWBALL EFFECT

As I stood in my third home, which had come quickly on the heels of the second home, looking outside at the Ferrari that had quickly come on the heels of my cherished Lambo, I felt a sinking sense of ennui. Mostly because Rehan had me making another video and a bird (a fucking bluebird) managed to fly into the living room because the back door to the veranda had been left open.

"My name is Hisham. Since I was thirteen, I've had the drive to be an entrepreneur. My motivation and drive were direct consequences of my mistakes and failures. Every mistake brought me one step closer because I knew what NOT to do."

"Bro, don't speak in capital letters."

God, this was getting old. And how did Rehan know that I spelled that in capital letters? "It's not wrong to be wrong because if *I* were wrong, my STEM school wouldn't be here today, creating patents and innovations nonstop."

Rehan turned the camera off and managed to compliment me in the only way he knew how: "That was so lame, bro."

I put up a discerning hand as my stomach went into a lurch. "Dude, I'm gonna puke. Please, not today. I'm just practicing for tonight." I checked my Rolex again, reminding Rehan who was boss. "I have to do this thing in, like, four hours."

"What is it, though?"

The event that Mr. Faizan had me speaking at felt like a cruel joke. "It's some kind of millionaire thing. I dunno."

"Like, talking in front of millionaires?"

"I guess."

Rehan lifted his brows like the villain Jafar. "Don't shit the bed!"

Shit got weird as *Aladdin* quotes came tumbling out. I shrugged. "Hey, I'm a street rat, remember? I'll improvise."

Rehan caught on to this quote far too quickly. "What would you wish for?"

"Well, there's this girl ..."[14]

We both froze and sat in a puddle of bro agony. How did we both know random lines from *Aladdin*? My Pakistani ancestors were rolling in their graves. Rehan clutched his Quran in utter despair.

---

14 · Ron Clements and John Musker, dirs., *Aladdin*, Walt Disney Feature Animation, 1992.

After just losing the man card that I'd not even received yet, I came clean. "I'm scared ... scared that I might shit the bed." It was perhaps the most honest thing I'd ever conveyed to Rehan.

In slow motion, as though in a scene from *The Matrix*, Rehan pulled a piece of paper from his back pocket. "Call her. Call *the one*."

The mother fucker had Maryam's number? I could have punched him. He'd said that she had no personality but then got her *number*? My fury prompted me to rip the piece of paper from his hand and serve justice in the best way that I could. "Yeah, bro. I will."

------------------ | MISFIT MOTIVATION | ------------------

If your bro has your girl's number, it's okay to be seriously pissed, but act upon the opportunity anyhow. No comment about the Aladdin quotes.

KITCHEN TALK

For once in my life, I wasn't seated on the kitchen floor speaking to Mr. Faizan; I was talking with the الهة (Goddess). I still curled my finger around the twisty cord while showing a nervous grin in my open-concept kitchen with a Viking range and oven.

"Who is this?" she asked.

"Um ... this is Allstate Insurance, calling about refinancing your home."

Absolutely nothing about this statement made sense, and I realized that I'd engaged in a crank call due to Outsider horror.

"What?"

I received the bro nod from Rehan and mustered my courage. "I'm totally joking. This is Hisham. Um ... Hisham Ahmad."

She paused on the other end as I felt my soul drift off into space. "Oh, hey, Hisham. What's up?"

I fist-pounded the air at receiving the coveted *what's up*. She hadn't given a declaration of love or devotion, but *what's up* was the gateway. It meant that Maryam wasn't opposed to speaking with me, even though the conversation went like this: "Did you see my Lambo?"

Rehan clasped the bridge of his nose and deeply inhaled. "Nuh, bro. Nuh."

"It's a very nice car," ة إله (Goddess) Maryam replied.

"Thank you. I'm enjoying it a lot."

"Why are you calling?"

"I have a big speech tonight, and I guess I'm feeling nervous and just wanted to embarrass myself with you first." I was reaching. Reaching!

"Well … why would that embarrass you? I think you'll do great."

Time stood still as the Misfit Mogul in me melted. "You're being so nice because I got crazy cars and houses and shit … *stuff*."

I heard her gorgeous laughter on the other end. "No, Hisham. I think you're very cool."

"Thanks, I gotta go." I quickly hung up the phone and watched as Rehan suffered from a teenage stroke. He literally fell to the floor and clasped his chest in pain. "Bro!"

I reached out my hands in compunction. "I couldn't speak anymore. It was too *hard*."

He winced. "I don't need that imagery, bro."

"No, asshole. I mean *difficult*. I didn't know what else to say, and I freaked out. I'm freaking out about everything!"

Rehan put a strong hand on my shoulder. "Bro, you have a watch box that lights up, and I think even has Siri installed."

"I thought of that. Yeah."

"You'll be victorious tonight. You already have been. You're moving up in life."

My heart instantly warmed, but where the hell was I moving up to?

──────────── | MISFIT MOTIVATION | ────────────

It's okay to tell the girl of your dreams that you're calling on behalf of Allstate Insurance when your Invisible persona freaks out It's also okay to head to a conference room at the Ritz and pray to Allah that you don't shit the bed

──────────────────────────────────

Yeah, I got bling, but having bling doesn't solve the world's problems. Solving the world's problems will definitely allow you to have bling. I'm at a place in life where I'm not afraid to indulge in the things that I want, and I've learned enough to know how to get it. I also know this: Money won't make you happy, per se, but there are things about having wealth that do make you happy. Being rich is frowned upon by some, but knowing *why* you want to be rich will help you to put in the extra work.

There is financial wealth as well as wealth of spirit. My pocketbook was getting larger as my spirit asked questions. Not to sound trite, but sometimes a heavy pocketbook gives you the freedom to ask questions. If you don't have money, then, bro, there's nothing wrong with you. If you want money, there's also nothing wrong with you. Life is a game of Choose Your Own Adventure, and everything that I was taught made me golden. Did this solve my challenges in life? Well ... I mean, it solved a few of them, but that's not to say that it solves every problem.

Outsider alert: money won't solve matters of the heart. Cue the romantic music.

Invisible Homework

- Let's go back to Kiyosaki. "Choose heroes and the power of myth."[15] At this point in the story, I felt like I was pretending—pretending to be my heroes. My financial heroes were Mr. Faizan and Dad. Everything they'd taught me was paying

15   Kiyosaki, *Rich Dad Poor Dad*.

off. Who are your financial heroes? Bro, it could be the guy who runs his own Domino's. Learn about him and act like him for a day. Eat his pizza, and talk to his CPA.

• His CPA better not be Shirley because she's mine.

Notes 'n' Stuff:

JOINING THE JET SET

Achieving success will put you in front of
powerful people Don't be afraid All
jet-setters are still Misfits at heart

At the Ritz-Carlton, Dallas, I hobnobbed with elite innovators, CEOs, and business tycoons. I worried over my speech and worried over the fact that Rehan wasn't here and that Mr. Faizan was wearing a better suit than me. He followed me around like a handler, and I didn't appreciate it. I was like a Pakistani Britney Spears, and Faizan was looking for the conservatorship.

As I was ushered from face to face, shaking hands and not knowing who the hell I was meeting, it occurred to me that I'd reached a new level of visibility. People knew about me. This was incredibly odd considering that I had been an Invisible Outsider my entire life, and all that had changed was the acquisition of cars, patents, and houses.

And Maryam talking to me on the phone …

"Hisham, I'd like you to meet one of the top leaders at Facebook," Mr. Faizan said.

The young guy in the hoodie put me at ease. He was older than me but had that Silicon Valley, I'm-super-young-and-successful vibe. "Cool car, man," he said. "I saw you roll in."

"Thanks, bro. I like it … I like it a lot."

This was when I realized that talking to the jet set was different from talking to UTD or even YouTube audiences. My need to fake confidence was now crucial. As I looked at the elaborate dining room with fine china and crystal glasses encircling the tables, it was clear that I'd dine well that evening, but I craved a Tupperware meal with Rehan in the quad.

—————————— | MISFIT MOTIVATION | ——————————

Becoming a millionaire at the age of seventeen opens a lot of doors and puts you in rooms with many important people Be yourself That's the person they want to meet

ABOVE AND BEYOND

The nameless host of the evening (I had no idea who he was because I was in a daze and couldn't remember anyone's name) announced, "Before we invite the inspiring Hisham Ahmad to the stage, let's first speak to his mentor, Mr. Faizan: computer scientist, entrepreneur, business owner, and NASA innovator."

The audience gave a polite golf clap, and I looked down at my roasted salmon in horror. I knew … I just knew this would go on for hours. Mr. Faizan was quite the raconteur.

He adjusted his tie and took a sip of water. "I suppose it's fitting that I stand here speaking of Hisham. There's much to say that he wouldn't be comfortable saying himself."

I feel death coming. Utter death.

"In truth, Hisham is very humble and keeps to himself. He has an insatiable mind. Let me tell you a story. We worked on an innovation at STEM, and everyone was happy with it, but then Hisham called me at 10 p.m. to share that he saw a problem that no one else had seen. I asked, 'What is the problem?'"

It was true that I'd called him at that late hour … He went on to describe my lockbox and how I was so anxious about the mortality of snakes and squirrels. To my amazement, the audience warmly laughed.

"Once he offered the solution, I said, 'That's brilliant, dude.'" (Yes, Mr. Faizan *duded* me in front of an audience of millionaires and billionaires.) "'How amazing that you thought of that!' We went through the patenting process, and Hisham was awarded his certificate far sooner than anyone could have imagined."

The audience supplied a more robust applause, and I perked up. Maybe I wasn't lame? Maybe Mr. Faizan wasn't lame? Perhaps we were both incredible! After purchasing several cars and houses, I still found it challenging to wrap my head around this lightning pace.

—— | MISFIT MOTIVATION | ——

Even at the Ritz, the salmon can be dry. Be prepared to have a PB and J when you get home

SEEING MYSELF FOR THE FIRST TIME

As Mr. Faizan continued, I got a bit weepy and hid it with an R-C monochrome napkin with a high thread count.

"Hisham came to me and said, 'I want to commercialize.' Earlier, we were only teaching *innovation* but not commercialization. Our STEM school did not have an entrepreneurship program. It was Hisham's idea. I said to him, 'Dude, innovation is one game, but commercialization, launching a start-up—these are entirely different games.'"

Yet again, Faizan *duded* me.

"I came to the realization that I wanted to play that game as well. He asked, 'What do we need?' I told Hisham that we needed a CPA, an office, investments, product designers, and a management consultant. We required everything, and we went through all the steps to get what we needed, finding investors and entrepreneurs. We built a company, incorporated it, and assigned kids as product designers."

Like in China …

"We now have ties with some of the best product designers in the world. They come to our STEM class, understand the products, and begin to do the research. Then the product design begins; it goes through one phase, a second phase, and then multiple other phases. How will the product look? How will it feel? How will it work? Sometimes what is patented will look slightly different through various phases of innovation."

Looking down at my barely touched fish, I went back in my mind as though it were a time machine. It was true; the relentless hard work and curiosity had transformed an Invisible kid into a Misfit Mogul.

The nameless host (he could have been Warren Buffett for all I knew) came to the podium and spoke. "That is fascinating. *Fascinating*, Mr. Faizan. How remarkable that a young man could achieve so much with such diligence." The lights rose over my head, and I was summoned. "Please, Hisham. Come onto the stage and speak."

As I walked to the stage on shaky legs, it felt like I was receiving an Oscar for the first movie I'd ever made. The host stepped aside, and I said into the microphone, "Thank you, Mr. Buffett."

The host appeared perplexed, and I think Mr. Faizan grasped his eyes in shame.

----------------- | MISFIT MOTIVATION | -----------------

It's important to memorize names, bro. I'm still bad at it, but I try to write them down on my napkins. Find a method that works for you. More importantly, give yourself a pat on the back sometimes. We often forget how hard we're working and how this effort drives our futures.

LIGHT BULB MOMENT

I glanced at my notecard as my head spun. Had I been ignorant of my achievements all along? Had the Outsider frustration and internal brooding blinded me to what I'd achieved? I pulled the microphone closer just as I saw Shirley come through the door at the back of the ballroom, wearing her knit sweater over a lovely skirt. I smiled to myself.

"Picture a world where every young mind is a seed, waiting to be nurtured. Our American school system has been watering these seeds, enriching us with knowledge. But the question is, are we growing in the right direction?"

Shirley fist-bumped the air.

"Let me share with you the story of Thomas Edison. The man who gave us light. He made one thousand *unsuccessful* attempts at inventing the light bulb. When a reporter asked him how it felt to fail one thousand times, Edison replied, 'I didn't fail one thousand times. The light bulb was an invention with one thousand steps.' Our schools have been successful in teaching us the steps, but they need to do more. They need to teach us how to … um"—sweaty palms—"navigate the failures, the dead ends, and the winding roads that lead us to our light bulb moments."

The audience was riveted, but for whatever reason, I cursed the seven-page report I had to write that night for English class the next day. *This shit never ends …*

I folded the notecard and used my real Hisham voice.

"Listen, I'll just say that STEM is kind of a new way of looking at life. We talk about Old School versus New School. The Old School is the system we're assigned to. The New School is the system that essentially innovates how we learn and what we *do* with knowledge. We're not prepped for success. Many people look down upon success and bling." (I couldn't believe that I used the word *bling*.) "But in truth, human nature craves success. Owning things that make us happy, sure, but also affording ourselves experiences in this one brief life."

From a distance, I envisioned Rehan holding the Quran to his heart in agony. *We live many lives*, he would have whispered.

"There can be ... um ... *many* other lives to come ..." At a front-row table, Mr. Faizan's face was wooden. "But we can seize this life now and believe in success, seek it when it's not guaranteed, and continue to believe in the value of our minds and spirits. Even at a young age, we can fight for the unthinkable, but first, we must learn how to do it and surround ourselves with those who take us there."

My throat went dry, and I felt a bit dizzy, but my mind drifted to the memory of the library lady, seeing me with my stack of books on that rickety table and scolding me to get out into the world. I guess I'd achieved just that.

The host, who was not Warren Buffett, came to the podium with a warm grin and spoke into the mic. "Hisham, I'm sure everyone in this room is curious as to what you've accumulated in your entrepreneurial endeavors."

He was being nice, but I knew he was talking money. "Twenty-five million, sir."

I watched as the audience collectively turned their heads to one another in awe.

─────── | MISFIT MOTIVATION | ───────

You can be at a fancy event and still worry about the homework you have to do when you get home

BRO-CATION

That night, as I tried to write my seven-page report from hell, Rehan endlessly failed at Nintendo while judging my emotional state.

"Bro, you need a vacation or something. You seem stressed."

I appreciated the sentiment. I was tired of school, tired of dreaming about the exoskeleton, and as Mikhail would confirm, I felt bored in STEM as well. I had a Lambo, a Ferrari, and three homes but an unacknowledged longing within, so I decided to open my heart to Rehan.

"I want to travel," I said.

"Where?"

"A place where I'm not the brown Outsider kid. I want to be the Outsider kid amid a sea of people who think white people are weird looking."

I watched as Rehan registered my words. "Bro, the Abdul guy said you can come to Dubai."

My mind wandered to the blue skies in the background of his Zoom call and how it looked so lush and bling-appropriate. I could show off there. Everyone else did. I could go skiing, go on safari, swim with the dolphins, or eat in that crazy flying restaurant. Still, a new thought came to mind. "I want to go to the motherland."

He appeared confused. "Russia?"

I shook my head in utter dismay. "Nah, bro. Pakistan."

─────── | MISFIT MOTIVATION | ───────

Staying connected with your roots is important, especially if those family and friends support you. The Misfit Mogul needs to stay grounded in their heritage. However, if these people do in fact suck, then just go to Dubai.

LIBRARY FUNK

The following day, I turned in my seven-page report, ditched history class, and came full circle to where this whole journey began. My Amazon Prime order had arrived in one day and was not stolen from my lockbox. A squirrel had been saved due to my efforts, but I was feeling pensive. I sat at the wobbly table. The glossy new copy of *Rich Dad Poor Dad* rested beside *Federal Income Taxation: A Law Student's Guide to the Leading Cases and Concepts*, Colin Wilson's *Outsider*, and *A Traveler's Guide to Pakistan* (which I didn't need but liked for the nostalgic pictures).

"Hisham," the library lady said, no longer folding her arms or scowling at me. "You are not in the quad for lunch, but I will let it pass this time."

This personality change was confusing. "Why is that?"

"Because you've proved yourself. You've proved that you can be a success."

Although I was flattered, the Misfit inside was pissed. I hadn't proved myself. Sure, speaking in front of a bunch of millionaires and then writing a seven-page paper had shown that I'd accomplished something in twenty-four hours, but this schedule was a Sisyphean effort that showed no end. I would long-game my success, and Mr. Kiyosaki would agree that this was a lifelong endeavor to keep working hard and not cry like a girl.

"Thank you, ma'am."

She sat beside me, clasping her thick fingers together. "I just hear so many marvelous things about what you've achieved." The library lady brought a palm to her chest. "I'm utterly delighted to know you."

I gazed out the library window, seeing my new white Porsche shining like a beacon in the parking lot. And still, I sat in the library with my Tupperware. This had been by choice. I had a special mission to accomplish.

"Why are you here today?" she asked. "All the kids want to see you. You're the talk of the town!"

I found this hard to believe, but I curtly answered, "There's something I need to do." I picked up the fresh copy of *Rich Dad Poor Dad* and placed it where it belonged, back in the 332.024 section.

She appeared momentarily stricken. "Did you steal it, Hisham?"

"Yes, Library Lady. And I'm grateful that I did."

| MISFIT MOTIVATION |

Just because you're a Mogul doesn't mean you're no longer a Misfit. It's important that you remain a deviant nonconformist throughout the process. Innovation requires you to study the rules and then break them.

MARYAM'S RAINBOW

After owning up to my misgivings in the library, I had two more tasks to accomplish. My backpack held a set of pastel markers and a set of primary colors. One was for ملاك (Angel) Maryam.

I didn't intend to stay in math class that day, but rather I'd perform the most important mission of all. There was no shame in ditching every class, thanks to my 5.0 GPA and my remarkable speech hosted by the guy who looked like Warren Buffett the night before.

As I stepped inside hell (the room was actually hot), Soraya Godzilla scrutinized me from behind her glasses before saying, "Hisham, I'm so glad you're here."

I could have replied with a witty and self-deprecating phrase. Instead, I walked straight to Maryam's desk. She gave me that gorgeous side glance before I placed the pack of pastel markers on her desk. The markers had sparkles in the ink, which I needed to analyze more so that I could create my own brand.

"These are for you," I said, stating what was profoundly obvious.

Her eyes lit up, and the class snickered at the exchange.

"That's … um … very nice, Hisham."

She'd *ummed* me, and that's how I gained confirmation that she would be my girl one day. "I'll soon make markers like this and innovate them so that the glitter ink is refillable." I froze, afraid that I'd said too much and that the Invisible Outsider floodgates had opened at the wrong time. I needed to harness the James Bond, the superhero—anyone but the tenderhearted Misfit who was now a millionaire and mildly embarrassed about it.

The math class guy who always sat beside her shrank in his chair, as though he'd lost a foot of height or a game of beer pong.

Maryam blushed and pulled out a pink marker from the package. "I can't wait to use these."

"I can't wait to see you do so."

———————— | MISFIT MOTIVATION | ————————

*Girls love markers I'm serious If you're looking
for a great gift that will make her feel seen,
buy her markers or one of those clicking
pens that has like fifteen different colors*

FULL SPEED AHEAD

As I awkwardly left math class, I had to wonder how much of this romantic interlude had only been in my imagination. I teetered as I walked to my Porsche, ready for my next baller moment of the day.

Clutching the steering wheel, I sped along (at a mildly legal pace) and listened to the Weeknd sing "Blinding Lights." Grown-ass men stared at me from other cars in fascination. I knew what they were thinking: *How did this kid earn that car? Did his dad buy it for him?*

No. I bought it, motherfucka!

I arrived at my father's CPA building to greet Shirley at just the right time. She was eating a Marie Callender's[16] pasta dish, so I at least saw some improvement in her dietary choices. I laid down the markers in primary colors.

"Is this for me?" Shirley asked.

"Yes, I wanted to give you a gift. These aren't my refillable markers, but the patent is in the mix."

Shirley appeared genuinely flattered until she replied, "Oh, Hisham, at this stage of the game, you could buy me diamonds!"

She wasn't far off by any stretch of the imagination.

"I just want to … um … thank you for believing in me. You never doubted me."

Shirley grasped my hand. "Young man, I need to do your taxes. Your father will not find as many deductions as I can."

I smiled to myself. Little did beloved Shirley know, my father could find every possible deduction. "That's nice. I think I got it." Not only did my father have the secrets, but I'd learned them myself.

"Gosh, I said that one day you'd become a millionaire. I just didn't know it would happen so quickly!"

In a moment of Misfit reflection, I replied, "Anyone can do it. You just have to know *why* and *how*."

————————— | MISFIT MOTIVATION | —————————

Take heed. Ladies love markers, but once they know your income, they'll request diamonds

---

16   No need for a footnote here, but I like it.

LEGAL ABUNDANCE

Seated in the office of attorney T-Rex, I was eager to have the last excursion of the day be done.

"Hisham, I summoned you here because there are many investors on board for your self-regulated, hypoallergenic door handles. This innovation is incredibly important during these challenging times."

The fact that he used the word *summoned* made this encounter extra cool.

"That's ... like, good news."

"Yes, this could turn into a multimillion dollar company. It seems as though you keep winning, Hisham." These words were kind, but T-Rex continued to stare stoically at his notebook bound in leather. "You need the law on your side throughout all of this. Any important innovation that you bring into the world can come with litigation, patent rights, incorporation, and a whole host of other steps and issues."

I was instantly bored and mildly annoyed. "I know this, sir."

"How do you know?"

"I've read *Letters to a Law Student: A Guide to Studying Law at University*." I'd memorized it ...

T-Rex placed his pen in his fancy leather penholder (was everything in this office leather?). "I see. You know so much more than I did at your age. We will have a bright future together."

Red flags were flying. It was true ... I could see it now. T-Rex also wished to retire in Dubai with my dad and Mr. Faizan. The Misfit in me struggled with trust, but still, the coming-of-age man knew that they all sincerely wanted to do for me what no one else could—to give me something grander than a fighting chance.

"Bet," I admitted.

"What do you wish to do now?" he asked.

"I'm feeling burned out," I replied. In reality, I was utterly exhausted and couldn't wrap my head around all the plates I had swirling in the air—another business, teaching STEM, three houses, millions of dollars, and a Lambo that was making funny noises. "I want a vacation."

"You can have anything you want, Hisham," he shared with avuncular seriousness.

"I'd …" The Outsider turned *insider* longed for the non-Russian motherland and a good plate of Grandma's nihari. "I'd like to go to Pakistan."

"That sounds very nice."

What I decided to share next had been eating away at my napkin-idea-strained mind. "I'd also like to go to Harvard, Yale, Stanford. I want to study law."

T-Rex appeared confused. "You don't need to, Hisham. You're a millionaire. You own businesses and real estate."

The mildly tortured Misfit Mogul realized something that day— he had a grander purpose. Still, suspicion was piqued. "You just want your ticket to Dubai, bro."

| MISFIT MOTIVATION |

One thing always leads to another (stay focused: you know what I'm talking about) One success leads to another. Through your exhaustion, continue dreaming about the future, but give yourself a break sometimes.

When I talked about bling, I said that money isn't everything, but there are tons of ways that it contributes to happiness—cars, trips, houses; it's just fun, bro! That being said, the jet set aren't necessarily the happiest people in the world, but many of them have a blast. After the success that I achieved, I was burnt out (and I'm still burnt out today). As I write this, I have one more year till I graduate from high school. I'm in the trenches with you.

The Misfit Mogul mindset asks you to look ahead while wallowing down in the present. It's not your fault that you have a ton of papers to write and you think you'll go insane. It's nearly impossible to escape the system unless you are homeschooled, but then you might turn out weird. Think out of the box and plan for the future by learning the real-world realities.

Although I desperately needed a break and a girlfriend, my mind was still spinning over *what's next?* In truth, I was thinking of being a lawyer. I dreamt of attending an Ivy League school to keep growing. Even though I was already exhausted, I discovered something about myself; I wanted to know what the next achievement would be. You'll find that hard work and success keep mutating into something new. That's because you're standing on the shoulders of what you've previously accomplished.

Invisible Homework

- In the flowchart on the next page, start with the very last box. Write down your biggest accomplishment to date. Now, work backward, naming five key steps that got you to where you are. See the milestones. This doesn't have to be huge. Maybe you learned how to make pizza from scratch (although that *is* huge), but notice the work that you put in.

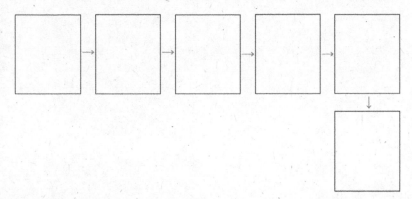

- Now, write down your next steps for that achievement. You can even pivot and choose a new achievement.

Notes 'n' Stuff:

(12)

THE END IS JUST THE BEGINNING

*We started from the bottom and
(awkwardly) arrived at the rooftop.*

When Mr. Faizan picked us up to go to the airport, he handed me an ice cream sandwich. I had three conflicting feelings about this:

1. *This was a downgrade of his affection*
2. *Faizan was trying to bond during the drive*
3. *I missed the swing set (I'd donated money to fix it)*

"This will be a remarkable trip, Hisham," Mr. Faizan proclaimed as he dad-drove the streets to Dallas/Fort Worth International. In the back seat sat my actual dad, who checked his phone the whole time. "I think it will give you some perspective and allow your brain to rest."

"My brain never rests," I flatly replied, eating my ice cream sandwich and imagining a sandwich bar where you choose from a variety of different cookies and ice cream flavors. I'd need to research this online to see if a similar establishment existed, and if it did, I'd need to find the flaws in their operational system so that I could improve upon it.

Okay, so yeah. I needed to rest my brain.

Faizan tightly gripped the steering wheel. "I've told you how proud I am, Hisham. I ..." Oh shit, he was choking up. "I think that this is only the beginning."

My heart warmed as I felt a wave of fatigue. Just the fucking beginning?

He continued, "So many people will miss you while you're gone: T-Rex, Shirley and the gang, Mountain Dew guy, popcorn guy, Library Lady, Math Godzilla, Alexis, the three Natalies, Rehan, and of course, myself."

I froze for what felt like five minutes. I even looked in the rearview mirror to see if my dad had clocked this. Was I going insane, or had Mr. Faizan memorized all the names in my head? I almost opened the door to the moving car so that I could bolt.

Still, I had my customary response. "Thanks, bro."

"And ألهة (Goddess) Maryam."

Oh, thank Allah! Now I didn't care that Faizan could read my mind (we'd been working on technology to accomplish just that) because he said that Goddess Maryam would miss me!

"He's only going to be gone for two weeks," my father muttered.

This was a huge blow. No longer was I the brown Greek hero Odysseus, traveling home after the Trojan War. I was just going to the slums of Pakistan for two weeks.

───────── | MISFIT MOTIVATION | ─────────

Mr. Faizan has been a dad of sorts. Robert T. Kiyosaki was a dad on paper. I essentially have three rich dads. Seek out your rich dads, my friends. They don't have to be blood related; they just need to teach you the truth and believe in you.

سفر (PAKISTAN BOUND)

I pretty much assumed that my dad only agreed to fly with me to Pakistan because

1. *I was now rich*

2. *His parents (my grandparents, duh) were there*

3. *We both needed a break from our* Rich Dad Poor Dad *odyssey*

As we waited for our Qatar Airlines flight to Jinnah International Airport, I ate a Cinnabon, gave in to the intense sugar rush, and contemplated the meaning of life, stating, "I'm excited to see Aziz and Amir."

"I am sure your cousins are excited to see you too," my father replied, still on his phone.

"This will be … um … fun. Grandma Bisma's cooking!" It was hard to admit that I thought of her as *Grandbisma*.

"Yes, I look forward to it as well."

I didn't have the heart to tell him that I looked forward to seeing beautiful Pakistani girls dressed in colorful kurtas.

I'd need to look the part and had come prepared, packing a *shalwar kameez* tunic. This would be a welcome respite from my polo shirts, which I was now convinced were the equivalent to a white person's disguise. I couldn't wait to appear as a poor Pakistani Misfit (without using any shameful *Aladdin* quotes).

Once our flight boarded, I promptly leaned into my Captain America neck pillow and slept for most of the twenty-hour duration, with brief intervals of standing, going to the restroom for the purpose of moving, and enjoying a four-course meal in business class, which was essentially sleep-eating class.

I dreamt of the exoskeleton design, and *I* needed that innovation to move once we landed. On the verge of fainting, I had a cough, indigestion, and mild fears that I might have been that guy who started screaming that an alien was on the wing. My dad was placid and calm as ever, so I probably hadn't been "that guy."

In a haze, I collected my bag and entered the screaming streets of Karachi. I quickly woke up to the sounds and smells, the bustling crowds, the littered streets, and the people who had no idea that I was a Misfit Mogul.

| MISFIT MOTIVATION |

Bro, if you go on a long flight, do whatever you must. Sleep, walk around, get drunk, or join the mile high club. I couldn't do the latter two because I was with my dad, but have a Misfit plan to survive.

GRANDBISMA OF THE SOUL: روح کی دادی آمنہ

At Grandbisma's table, my eyes continued to gently close. I needed sleep, but there was no way I would miss this experience. We were seated on her *dastarkhān* eating space. My cousins Aziz and Amir flanked me on each side. These guys looked suave and probably had secret girlfriends, which made me question the American dream.

Gentle, beautiful Grandbisma implored, "کھاؤ، کھاؤ!" *(Eat, eat!)*

The nihari might have been more stunning than Maryam. (But Maryam's lips probably tasted better. So sorry. Conjecture). The steaming dish of slow-cooked beef, lamb, and chicken; the biryani rice; the garlic naan ... For the entirety of this meal, I'd no longer be a millionaire, Misfit, or Outsider; I'd be a hungry kid in utter bliss.

As I reached for my spoon with my left hand, Dad smacked my wrist. "Wrong, son."

"Fuck."

He gave me the death stare.

"Shit … I mean, fuck. No! I'm sorry …"

Oh, god. It was poor etiquette to use the left hand to grasp cutlery in Pakistan. I'd utterly forgotten and thanked Allah that Grandbisma didn't know much English.

The meal continued, thanks to my father not ending my life and the contented laughs from my cousins.

Grandbisma said, "آپ مالدار ہیں.۔" (*You are wealthy.*)

"She says you are loaded," I-probably-have-a-hidden-girlfriend Aziz translated.

Here we go. It was game time. I had to do my best. "میں پیسے کرتا ہوں." (*I'm a very wealthy young man who dreams of future prosperity.*)

"Bro, you just say, 'I money do,'" I'm-definitely-getting-laid-by-twenty-different-women Amir laughed.

Although this gaff was shameful, I was flattered that I'd been *Bro*-ed in Pakistan.

———————— | MISFIT MOTIVATION | ————————

It's important to learn the language of your people. Learn it early. Don't offend your grandmother. She'll think you're a lost cause.

AN INVISIBLE STROLL

After dinner, I wished to clear my head and get a taste of Pakistan. The roads were paved with dirt, and run-down cement buildings populated my left side while slum encampments bordered my right.

Although my modest gray shalwar kameez was the opposite of Misfit Mogul attire, I still felt high class in contrast to my surroundings. Babies cried. Countless lines of drying clothing loomed overhead. There was also music. Qawwali (قوالی), the sound of the Chishti Sufis, filled the night sky.

The colors and aromas piqued my senses, and for a fleeting hour of strolling, I forgot about my mansions and cars. I didn't even miss them (oddly, I did miss my watches). I wished that Rehan was here in this moment of humble Outsider anonymity, but I also kinda didn't. He'd fuck it all up somehow.

The life that I witnessed around me was so simple and yet so strained; impossible to imagine that people lived like this day in and day out. I was nearly brought to tears witnessing their strife and anguish until I saw a woman in a lovely black hijab who looked like Maryam. I ran to her, due to maniacal instinct and teenage hormones, and proceeded to give her the shock of her life.

"Hello!"

"کیا کر رہے ہو تم؟" she asked. (*What are you doing?*)

Oh, god. Here we go with the floodgates.

"مجھے لگتا ہے کہ آپ خوبصورت ہیں ہاں." This roughly translated to *I think you beautiful yes.*

She modestly pulled the side of her hijab farther across her face. "میں تم سے بات نہیں کر سکتی۔" I think she said *I cannot talk to you.*

All right, it was the moment of truth. "میں وعدہ کرتا ہوں میں امیر آدمی ہوں." I could have just thrown my wallet at her. "ہوں." My response, *Me rich man I promise*, was a mixture of Christian Grey and Elmo.

"ہیں فٹ مس ایک آپ," she exclaimed before running away. (*Misfit!*)

And there it was … some girl in Pakistan called me a Misfit.

Never run up to a girl and state that you're rich This is so desperate, dude It's not gonna work You have to finesse her, even if you're the richest guy in the country

THE ROOFTOP

After my stroll was done, my father and I sat atop Grandbisma's roof and gazed out at the chaotic streets. These rooftops were meant for pedestrians to cross over and travel the city. As some random dude passed behind us, I felt a strange violation of space and property. Had it been one of my mansions, I would have Tasered him.

"There's a story I must tell you," my father said. I was all ears, knowing that this was a father-and-son-holding-beers moment. Except that if I had a beer, he'd hang me. "I was born in these slums. My father, your grandfather, won a game show." He smiled to himself. "This supplied a lottery ticket for our entire family to move to America."

"Like *Slumdog Millionaire*," I inappropriately replied.

On the other side of the world, I saw Mr. Faizan roll his eyes.

My father persevered through this Misfit ill-timing. "Let's be serious for a moment, Hisham." His eyes glistened, and I froze. Rarely had I seen my father in an emotional state. He pulled a napkin from his pocket and dabbed his eyes. "I was given a ticket to the American dream, son. I worked very hard and I … I have pushed you to do the same. To escape a place like this—a place where there is no future."

I pulled a napkin from my own pocket. It had a sketch of a more humane slum encampment. "So, it's just the money then? That's the American dream?" Yes, it was all true. I was pushed to the brink to make money. The American dream was temporary until the Dubai conspiracy theory came to fruition.

"No, Hisham." He motioned toward the adjacent building standing seven stories in height. "Your grandmother owned that school. It was the only reason she stayed in the slums. She could have gone elsewhere. But she cared. She cared about education and had built a legacy, the legacy that you now enjoy."

Off in the distance, fireworks went off, but not the Fourth of July kind. They were made of highly lethal gunpowder, helping the rooftops of Pakistan look even more like a war zone. Behind us, a kid my age ran past, holding a giggling girl's hand. When he tripped over the wires of the rooftop, my only thought was *Relatable, bro*.

A moment of Misfit indignation arose. I looked out and cupped my hand, holding an imaginary father-son beer. "You can do anything you want here. Everyone is so poor; no one cares what you do."

"And why is that important to you?"

I brought the napkin to my eyes. "Dad ..." My fake beer hand shook. "I want to be a kid. I always did. What is this American dream? I've learned so much, yes. I have wealth and all that. But I can be a Misfit here," I said, watching the stumbling kid take the girl's hand again before running from roof to roof below the starry night sky.

"You can be a Misfit anywhere, Hisham." I'm pretty sure his next statement was solely in my imagination. "But I will kill you."

Through my embarrassing tears, I steadily replied, "Dope."

"But the fact of the matter is"—Dad's voice cracked—"you're becoming a man. The man"—he reached over, his brown eyes reflecting the dangerous fireworks from the slum rooftops—"the man I always wished to be."

He cleared his throat and walked away, but I understood why. It was too much for him. I stood and approached the edge of the roof, the fireworks now exploding in a crescendo of someone-is-gonna-go-to-the-ER beauty.

The man my father always wished to be? The American dream?

The Misfit Mogul was pissed and inspired, tired and wide awake. Down below, a man walked past wearing an exoskeleton, a package was delivered to a lockbox, and a young girl strolled along with refillable markers. A bluebird landed on my shoulder and didn't take a crap, but most importantly, the streetlamp dimmed, making the moon more visible while helping people sleep at night.

I pulled my napkins from my pockets and released them, watching as they billowed into the sky. Somewhere across the world, Mr. Faizan was up late, sketching a satellite that could make it to Pluto even though it was no longer a planet, Rehan slept with his Quran as though it were a stuffed animal, and فرشتہ (Angel) Maryam gazed up at the stars—the same stars that I looked up at now. (I'd pay millions to name one after her.)

The American dream ...

I contemplated it for a bit. Had I achieved it, and was my life any easier because of that achievement? No, on both accounts. I still had crazy amounts of homework, SAT prep, and a continuous existential crisis. Did I regret any of the hard work I'd put in? Certainly not. There would be a lifetime of hard work and deep thinking, innovation, and starbursting my brains out.

The continuous fireworks popped like my nerve endings as I worried about it all. College (burst!), adulthood (burst!), love (burst!), the realities of life (burst!). Everything exploded inside me as I realized that Mr. Faizan's "New School" was the school within myself. The school of choice and determination in the face of a world that teaches you to be Invisible. برائے مہربانی اے خدا (Please, oh God), make it the school of connection, the school of Maryam!

The lively, raw nature of Pakistan finally helped me to understand what the fucking hell a New School was! Outrageous fortitude. My mind, imagination, and thoughts always pushing the boundaries. The school of my father, always working toward a life that sets you free. Determination in the face of setbacks and napkin ideas filling your pockets. Most importantly, witnessing the beauty of the slums, the rich energy of courage.

The New School sets you apart from Mountain Dew guys (even though I still face those). It's the New School of Shirleys, Faizans, Ralphs, and caring/scary librarians who push you out into the world. In essence, the school that you find for *yourself* taught by rich moms and dads, in both mind and spirit.

As Grandbisma stepped onto the roof, a dish of sweet rabri in her hands, she used impeccable English: "Hisham, get off of roof!"

"مجھے یہاں اچھا لگتا ہے," I replied. (*I like it here.*) "I can be Invisible."

"آپ پوشیدہ نہیں ہیں۔" (*You're not Invisible.*) "میں آپ کو دیکھ سکتی ہوں۔". (*I see you.*)

I smiled to myself, incredibly touched. "Thanks, Grandbisma."

She pointed her finger in the air. "But you still Misfit!"

End of story. But the *visible* Misft thought, "Here we start …"

| MISFIT MOTIVATION |

It's always the beginning and never the end. Keep working your ass off while you're tired, confused, bored, or doubting yourself. There's a reason why you're on this journey, bro. You have an insatiable need to accomplish something, and if you are the child of first-generation Americans, your mom or dad holds a whip. There's a reason for this. They know what life can be like elsewhere, and they want the very best for you.

CONCLUSION

Bro, you read a motherfucking book. (As I stated throughout these pages, *bro* is also applicable to girls, and I'm sure you're all beautiful and wicked smart.) For the dudes, I'm sure you're *not* beautiful, but eventually you'll stand a chance with the smart chicks. Thanks for coming along on this journey, and as I said, each chapter of your life is always a new beginning.

If you didn't read this book and skimmed to the conclusion, I'll break it down for you:

1. Finding solutions to problems makes you an innovator.

2. Learn "New School" stuff at an early age: finance, business, entrepreneurship.

3. Being a loner is doable when you set your imagination free

4. Find your rich dads, even if they didn't provide the sperm (so sorry!)

5. Use your voice, and step out of your comfort zone

6. Avoid Natalies and choose Shirleys

7. Always trust amazing friends like Rehan and mentors like Mr. Faizan, even if they annoy you

8. Stay away from bluebirds.

9. Dude, find the right books, like **Rich Dad, Poor Dad** (and this one, of course!)

10. Above all else, trust that as an Invisible Outsider, you can always transform into a Misfit Mogul with hard work and dedication, no matter your age.

11. Bonus: You're doing better than you think.

Invisible Homework

Class is dismissed. In your notes, write about random shit that excites you.

Notes 'n' Stuff:

CONTACT ME

LinkedIn:
www.linkedin.com/in/hisham-ahmad-9873b0247

Email:
hisham.the.Misfit@gmail.com

Instagram:
@hishamahmadofficial

And all handwritten love letters can be sent to:
Hisham, My Boo
555 Republic Dr.
Plano, TX 75074